THE COMPRE___ GUIDE TO FATHERS' RIGHTS

by
Ronald L. Isaacs, J.D.
Attorney at Law

complete texts of

THE GUIDE TO FATHERS RIGHTS

HOW TO MINIMIZE SUPPORT

FIGHTING FALSE ALLEGATIONS

WITH NEW CASE WINNING COURTROOM "TRICKS OF THE TRADE"

complete with sample pleadings & forms

The author: Ronald L. Isaacs, *Juris Doctor*
GUEST FATHERS' RIGHTS SPEAKER ON THE O'REILLY FACTOR, MSNBC NEWS, AND THE QUEEN LATIFAH TV SHOWS. FOUNDER OF THE FATHERS RIGHTS FOUNDATION,
Admitted to the Illinois and Federal bars.

THE FATHERS RIGHTS FOUNDATION
http://www.fathers-rights.com

Library of Congress Control Number: 2006940603
ISBN: 978-0-9741095-3-4
Printed in the United States by Morris Publishing
3212 East Highway 30
Kearney, NE 68847
1-800-650-7888

FOREWORD

TRUE HORROR STORIES

John's wife of twelve years disappears with his two daughters, ages 4 and 8. John has no idea where his children are. John is served with a protective order preventing him from coming near his wife or children. He had no notice of the hearing on whether the order should have been entered. He finds out that his daughters are in a women's center run by admitted lesbians and from across the street, sees a lesbian carrying one child with her hand on the little girl's private areas. Police are called to remove the irate father. Nothing is done about the lesbian's acts. Later, after a court hearing finally allows John access to his children they repeat what they have been told: "We don't need any men in our lives."

Bill kisses his little girl and goes to work without knowing that he will not be able to see her for two weeks and only after a court battle to grant temporary visitation. After Bill leaves, his wife goes to a county circuit clerk and obtains a fill-in-the-blank request for a protective order. Without even having to allege any physical threat of violence she obtains a judge's signature on the order. The order prevents Bill from coming near his home or children for at least 14 days. The wife then reports to her feminist lawyer who opens negotiations for property rights in a divorce while effectively holding the child hostage. To keep pressure on Bill, the lawyer proceeds to delay in every way possible a hearing which would establish temporary custody and visitation.

Ted never marries Alice, she becomes pregnant and they break up. Alice refuses to put Ted's name on the birth certificate or even let him see his little boy. Alice's mother files to adopt the child and Ted must file a paternity action asking to pay for the child's care and custody or visitation rights. Alice and her mother falsely claim the child has physical problems and convince the judge to allow Ted short visits only in the mother's home. Only after lengthy court battles over access to health records and temporary visitation rights is Ted allowed regular visitation as is his right guaranteed by federal and state law .

Roger returns home to find his wife and children and their clothing missing. For two years he searches for his children. After finally locating them through a tip from his wife's sister, he drives to a nearby state to return his children. He carries a court order authorizing him to return the children to his home. Tipped off by a courthouse employee, his wife runs to a nearby women's center where they refer her again to an underground network of feminists who secret women and their children from the children's fathers. Later, after another lengthy search Roger has his wife arrested for kidnaping and obtains custody of his children. Roger's wife and a women's center employee go to prison for kidnaping. At no time had Roger physically abused his wife or children.

Joan tells Bob she wants a divorce. Bob's friends are not up on fathers' rights and tell him normal visitation is every other weekend and that he has no chance for custody. Bob rolls over and gives Joan everything she wants so the children won't be deprived of their lifestyle. Bob's relationship with his children steadily deteriorates and Joan won't allow one more minute of visitation than the court order requires. Joan becomes overbearing and even controls telephone access to the children. Bob must spend a great deal of money to file for the increased visitation that he should have had all along. The children have been mentally abused by their mother's denying them a full relationship with their father and later grow to hate their mother for criticizing their father and interfering with visitation.

For many years divorced fathers docilely accepted their former wife's destruction of the relationship between the father and his children . No longer do fathers have to accept vindictive mental abuse or the damage done to their children's emotional stability. No longer is mental child abuse tolerated by our legal system.

Included in this guide are excerpts from Statutes and cases commonly used to fight for fathers' rights. If your attorney is not experienced in this area, give him a copy of this guide: *it may mean the difference between misery and happiness for your future.* Recent changes in law redefine the child's best interest in a manner to protect the father's rights. Illinois law is typical of the advancements made to protect both the parent's and the child's rights and is used herein as an example. Many states have come to realize the benefit to the child and society of preserving the father-child relationship after divorce and have adopted similar laws. Links to other states' laws and international resources are listed under "Internet Resources."

A new addition to this Guide is **TRICKS OF THE TRADE** interspersed throughout this guide**.** An example:

TRICK OF THE TRADE

If you argue that your spouse is unfit because her own pleadings and actions try to minimize vice maximize your time with the children while your pleadings ask for maximum involvement of both parents, you place your spouse in a legal box. She will either increase her offers or look foolish trying to explain to a cross examiner why she should have more time with the children than you and would run a serious risk of losing or not obtaining custody. Either way, you better your position and minimize emotional damage to the children. Even if you don't win custody, you will enjoy much more visitation than fathers usually are awarded. These tactics have actually been proven in the courtroom in custody /visitation/support litigation by Attorney Isaacs.

TABLE OF CONTENTS

CHAPTER 1 A NEW APPROACH TO FATHERS' RIGHTS

Society is finally recognizing the importance of fathers in the development of healthy, well-adjusted children. Children from fatherless homes are committing violence towards other children on an unprecedented scale. States are passing more father-friendly laws, and courts are awarding more fathers custody. One state, Illinois, is becoming "father-friendly" and we use that state's laws herein and encourage adoption of similar laws and cases by other states, countries and jurisdictions. Many states and countries now have similar laws, some examples of which appear in the appendix.

Amendments to the ILLINOIS MARRIAGE and DISSOLUTION of MARRIAGE ACT, The Illinois Supreme Court's Eckert decision, In re Marriage of Eckert, 119 IL. 2d 316,327, (1988), and subsequent cases decided and laws passed as recently as 1998 mandated a changed approach to custody and visitation determination in Illinois. Prior practices of awarding or restricting visitation and allowing removal of children from a state where the father resides should be, and have been, re-evaluated in light of these amendments and subsequent changes in law.

The amendments included securing the **maximum involvement and cooperation of both parents** in the child's welfare among the purposes of the Illinois Marriage and Dissolution of Marriage Act : 750 ILCS 5/102 (7):

Purpose:

(7) secure the maximum involvement and cooperation of **both** parents regarding the physical, mental, moral and emotional well-being during and after litigation.

TRICK OF THE TRADE

*This means that **ALL** statutes in the act must be interpreted with this goal in mind! This, or a similar purpose clause, may be found in most states' and countries' divorce laws and is your **starting point** in any legal argument.*

The amendments further re-defined best interest of the child to include a **presumption** for the maximum involvement and cooperation of both parents in the child's ongoing welfare.

750 ILCS 6/602(8)(c). Best Interest Defined:

The Court **shall presume** that the maximum involvement and cooperation of **both** parents regarding the physical, mental, moral and emotional well-being of their child is in the best interest of the child.

TRICK OF THE TRADE

*Having a presumption in your favor means you **do not have to prove** a right to maximum involvement, the person opposing maximum involvement must prove that it is not in the child's best interests, a very difficult task in light of many cases upholding this presumption. Again this presumption appears in many states' and countries' statutes or has developed through case law from cases that have been appealed. **Don't fall into the trap of being defensive** .The presumption is on your side! Argue it aggressively!*

DOES THE MOTHER ALWAYS GET CUSTODY?

Feminists have brainwashed women into thinking divorce is a lark, a simple procedure in which they get everything the poor slob of a husband has. Women's groups actively try to break up families and encourage divorce without telling women of how their entire future will be adversely affected and their children's emotions permanently damaged. Your spouse probably labors under the delusion that she has a superior right to your children. Do not accept this outdated premise! Illinois law is typical in how this premise was completely repudiated years ago.

"There is no longer a presumption in child custody disputes that the mother is necessarily a better custodian for young children." In Re Marriage of Milovich 434 NE 2d 81, 105 Ill. App 3d 596 (1982).

There were also doubts raised about the constitutionality of presumptively denying custody to one of admittedly fit parents: See King vs. Vancil, 34 Ill. App. 3d 831, 341, N.E. 2d 65 (5th Dist. 1975)

TRICK OF THE TRADE

When you stand up for your rights (including custody), spouses who think they can would run over you, take your kids, house and money suddenly face the possibility that they may lose custody and be required to pay child support. Suddenly they become more reasonable. ***Do not begin settlement negotiations by being reasonable. Demand everything just like she does!*** *In negotiations you can only compromise down . If your first offer is reasonable, where do you go from there? If you do not ask for sole custody several of the tactics in this book will not be as effective.* ***ALWAYS*** *file for custody, even in support matters.*

A NEW TEST FOR CUSTODY

The Illinois Marriage Dissolution Act was amended to add a new test for custody – the ability of the custodial parent to foster a relationship between the child and the non-custodial parent. See 750 ILCS 6/602(a)(8) for the test (BEST INTERESTS DEFINED, copy in appendix).

"The willingness and ability of each parent to facilitate and encourage a close and continuing relationship between the other parent and the child." 750 ILCS 6/602(a)(8)

This new test has been adopted in many states and countries and has resulted in many changes of custody from mothers to fathers because of mothers' refusals to obey court orders granting visitation rights. If your state or country does not have this statutory standard of evaluating whether a person is fit for custody, it may be found in case law. It is, however, a common sense test that **you should argue aggressively**. Many entire custody cases are won on this sole test. Careful records of visitation denials must be kept to effectively use this test for custody.

CAUTION

Visitation orders MUST contain specific days, dates and times to protect your rights to obtain contempt orders against an un-cooperative ex-wife. An order granting only REASONABLE visitation is an order effectively granting NO visitation without your ex's consent or without expensive litigation.

TRICK OF THE TRADE

Pleadings requesting only limited visitation are the best evidence of an unwillingness to facilitate! Use those pleadings as an example in your closing argument. Argue: "My client seeks equal time for the parents. Mrs. X seeks to limit the father's time to every other weekend. Mrs. X's pleadings ... (lift up her pleadings).. and arguments before this court ...(see cross exam of parent requesting to limit time which follows)... are the ***best*** *evidence of her unwillingness to further a close and continuing relationship between the child and the father!"*

LOUISIANA'S APPROACH

R.S. 9:335. Joint Custody Decree and Implementation Order

A. (1) In a proceeding in which joint custody is decreed, the court shall render a joint custody implementation order except for good cause shown.

(2) (a) The implementation order shall allocate the time periods during which each parent shall have physical custody of the child so that the child is assured of frequent and continuing contact with both parents.

(b) To the extent it is feasible and in the best interest of the child, physical custody of the children **shall be shared equally.**

JOINT CUSTODY

Studies prove a child's need for significant and continuing contact with both parents after divorce. If you and your spouse are both reasonable and cooperative a judge will often grant joint custody. However, if there is any animosity evidenced, judges will usually deny joint custody. Beware, however, of any joint custody agreement that is vague and does not give specific details of the agreement. Many times these agreements fall apart when the ex re-marries and attempts to make her new spouse (or boyfriend) the daddy of your children or when you re-marry and she resents your new spouse!

The ideal joint parenting arrangement often arises when the spouses work different shifts and trade the children at shift change.

Judges sometimes consider the Joint parent who is designated as the residential parent, or receiving child support, to effectively be the custodial parent. This may make joint custody a sham. If possible, make sure you are named the residential parent or insist that neither parent is named a residential parent nor primary parent. True joint custody would be an allocation on 50/50 as to the time the child spends with each parent. If that is the situation, there is no logical reason to pay child support since each parent is equally responsible for support and each has the child 50% of the time. In practice this seldom happens but it can be used as an argument for paying a lowered amount of support to a spouse with a lower income. Often, the mother "sells" the father joint custody in exchange for undisputed child support.

TRICK OF THE TRADE

It might be better to designate this arrangement as alimony vice support so as not to give an impression of custody in the receiving party and also so that payments may be terminated upon her marriage or cohabitation. Alimony payments would also be deductible.

BEST INTERESTS OF THE CHILDREN

Best interests of the children is not best interests of the children! Forget your common sense and feelings. Best interests of the children is a legal concept and is defined by case law and sometimes by statutes. To argue what is in the child's best interests, **you must know how your state laws or courts have defined best interests of the child**. Once you know what the standards applied and definitions are, **you must frame your legal arguments and case around those definitions**.

In Illinois, best interests are defined by eight paragraphs in a statute (see page 97). If you argue about something that is not included in those eight paragraphs you are wasting your and the court's time.

TRICK OF THE TRADE

In his opening argument, a good attorney will pull out the statute or case and go down the list of "tests" or factors deemed controlling by statute or case law. With the statute in his hand, he covers the factors deemed controlling by statute or case law one by one in his examinations and cross examinations of both parties. In his closing argument, he then points out the differences between the parties as to each of those factors. During the case he will argue that anything else brought up is irrelevant and inadmissable. This tactic often keeps an honest judge honest and frames the arguments to your advantage.

If your state has no defining statute you must search for cases under the keyword "best interests". In your opening statement to the Court you must establish what factors should be considered based on cases already decided. This sets up the ground rules and allows you to keep out irrelevant or possible harmful information.

Normally any alleged prior conduct of a parent that does not affect the relationship between the child and the parent is irrelevant. The original grounds for divorce is almost always irrelevant. Marijuana usage and cohabitation have been ruled irrelevant. It can be argued that alleged abuse of the spouse is not relevant to the relationship between the alleged abuser and the child, that there is no evidence that abuse of the mother would lead to abuse of the child (even if the "false" allegation was true). Non-payment of child support is VERY relevant and **if you haven't been paying promptly according to any court order you are doomed to lose absent good evidence the child is endangered by the other parent.** If no order exists and the other parent has been taking care of the child most of the time during the separation, voluntary payment of some money and expenses and clothing purchases makes you look good to the court.

TRICK OF THE TRADE

Sometimes you can "buy" time with the kids during the pre-trial period by paying the wife support but keeping the kids most of the time yourself. When your wife asks for custody and child support you can cross examine her as to why she hasn't voluntarily paid you any support. This makes her look bad as to custody. It can then be argued she sold the children to you for so much a month!

TRICK OF THE TRADE

Having pictures of a child-safe bedroom set up and equipped with toys for the children shows the court you are serious in your quest for custody. If necessary, you sleep on a couch to provide the child his or her own room. Girls' rooms should be separate from boys. If you can get pictures of a messy or dirty spouse's house or a dangerous environment, these are very effective. Have these pictures blown up at a copy place to at least 11"x 14".

MEDIATION

Often a judge will order mediation by a third party. This is non-binding and usually can resolve some issues, saving you litigation expenses on issues on which you agree . Cooperate with the mediators since they often have the judge's ear, but do not be bullied into giving up your basic rights. Often these mediators do not know the extent of a father's rights and will attempt to get you to settle for the old "every other weekend" visitation standard, with the mother having custody. Especially beware of young female mediators and non-lawyer mediators. Many mediators are social workers with no idea of how the law reads. Some are courthouse hangers-on who were, or are, involved with women's centers and are closet (or open) feminists. Usually, you may choose from a list of mediators. Become familiar with the reputation and qualifications of the persons on the list before accepting any mediator. **As a rule of thumb, avoid female mediators**. Try to select a male who has been divorced.

JUDGES

Some states allow you to disqualify the first judge assigned to the case if no hearings have been held. Make sure your attorney knows how the judge assigned rules and **as a rule of thumb, never accept a female judge** unless you know from someone else's personal experience that she is fair to men. Try to get a divorced male judge and your chances of success will skyrocket.

NEVER, NEVER contact or communicate with a judge outside the courtroom. You will blow your case. It scares a judge to death to receive a letter or be approached because several judges have been stalked and killed. Never speak in court unless you are testifying and do not react to testimony by muttering or using excessive body language. Ask all questions of the judge through your attorney.

TRICK OF THE TRADE

If you win your case, IMMEDIATELY leave the courthouse so the hearing cannot be re-convened or something new raised as an issue. The same is true of any mediation or negotiation meeting. Often you will negotiate at the courthouse just before a hearing. If you like the results, go directly to a judge and have the decision recorded to make it binding and then leave ASAP. Do not stay and talk!

THE GUARDIAN AD LITEM

The court may appoint a GAL to represent the child in custody or visitation cases. The GAL is usually an experienced attorney known for fairness, whose fees may be split by the parties or offered to be paid by the party asking a GAL be appointed. The GAL will interview all parties and witnesses and make his recommendation to the judge. The judge will give great weight to the GAL's recommendations. Your attorney will usually be given a veto over any selection for GAL1 and you should be very careful not to allow a non-lawyer social worker act as a mediator or GAL, as is sometimes allowed in certain states.

A GAL should also be appointed to represent the child in cases where an unwed father is barred from claiming paternity of his child after a statute of limitations has run. The case below shows how far an appellate court will go to ensure a child has involvement with both parents, even though the father was admittedly late in filing a petition to determine paternity and his parental rights.

> "The trial court erred in not appointing a Guardian Ad Litem when it was apparent to the trial court that the defendant did not wish to promote the child's interest in visitation with and child support from her father. The trial court had an obligation under these circumstances to appoint a Guardian Ad Litem, therefore the case should be remanded for an appointment of a Guardian Ad Litem for defendant's child." Majidi v. Palmer, 530 N.E. 2d 66, 175 Ill. App. 3d 679 at 685 (1988) (almost verbatim quote).

CHAPTER 2 DEFEATING DIRTY DIVORCE TACTICS

PARENT ALIENATION SYNDROME

Often shortsighted and abusive mothers will try to turn children against their father. The mentally abused children sometimes develop "Parent Alienation Syndrome." Gordon B. Plumb, Ph. D., recently published a book **Humanizing Child Custody Disputes**, Carbondale, Ill. (foreword by Congressman Glenn Poshard). Chapter VIII deals with Parent Alienation Syndrome, defined as:

> "a disturbance in which children are preoccupied with depreciation and criticism of a parent; denigration that is unjustified and/or exaggerated."

Furthermore,

> "Parent Alienation syndrome is caused by the conscious or unconscious acts of one parent brainwashing or programming a child against the other parent and if allowed to continue for over a year, there is a strong likelihood that any meaningful relationship between the child and the "hated" parent is impossible until at least the child becomes an adult. The irony of Parent Alienation Syndrome is that the child's feelings are most often the opposite to what is expressed through Parent Alienation Syndrome and the "preferred" parent is more often feared then preferred." (pp. 71).

Plumb cites Richard Gardner's writings as authority that in cases where one parent is fanatical in their animosity, **immediate placement of the child with the "hated" parent is essential to avoid irreparable psychological damage to the child** and that it is usually preferable for the "hated" parent to have custody.

Doctor Plumb further recommends no contact between the child and the "preferred" parent from one to a few months to reestablish the bonds between the "hated" parent and the child without interference (pp. 72), **and that any telephone contact between the "preferred" parent and the child be supervised** while the parents and child undergo professional counseling.

Proving PAS requires good record keeping and witnesses. Expert testimony by a psychologist who has examined the child is required and a motion for such an exam should be made early in the litigation. Make sure the psychologist you select accepts PAS as a true syndrome. Some psychiatrists refuse to acknowledge it exists but call the same symptoms different names.

TRICK OF THE TRADE

If you cannot afford to hire a psychologist, file several pleadings throughout the litigation objecting to you ex's conduct that is depriving you of time with the children and causing the children emotional harm. Also motion for an in-camera hearing of the children alone with the judge in his chambers, alleging that it is necessary because she is attempting to brainwash the children and the children would be intimidated by testifying in their mother's presence.

TRICK OF THE TRADE

Beware of having the child counseled by social workers. Most are feminists and will shoot the father down every time. Often they interview the mother first and for a long period of time and then interview the father for a few minutes after their mind is already made up. If social workers are involved, make sure you see them before your spouse does and that it is during a period when you have the child. If the interview is in your home (best) make sure everything is child-proof. Discuss the child's best interests, NOT your rights! Their favorite trick is to say you are more concerned about your rights than the child's future.

COURTROOM CONDUCT

The hostility of one parent may come out in court under skillful cross examination. The party who loses her or his cool on the stand or at his table loses, ***period***. If your spouse becomes angry or vindictive or lies during her questioning or mumbles or covers her mouth with her hand, or interrupts testimony with comments, your chances for winning increase.

Say " yes, sir" and "no, sir". Be calm and polite to everyone including the lawyer harassing you with questions. Look the judge in the eyes when answering questions. **Never lie.**

TRICK OF THE TRADE

Admit your wrongs but repent *and say how you've changed or gotten counseling. Bring up any bad thing you know your ex is going to use* ***before*** *your ex does and explain it away. This increases your credibility and pops her attorney's balloon.*

Dress like you are going to Sunday School, blue suit and white shirt and conservative tie. The same goes for your attorney. Get a haircut (no pony tails) and shave off any beard or mustache. Don't wear any glasses that are tinted or tint in the sun. You want direct eye contact with the judge! You really do want to enhance your chances of winning, don't you? You are playing for keeps here. This is no time to exert your individuality.

You are not a skillful cross examiner. Get a good lawyer with a reputation for being a ***shark****--a fighter who uses the cross examination and tactics in this book. Make sure you spend several hours with him the day before the hearing. Make sure he is up on all the facts so he can catch your ex lying and can be prepared with physical exhibits.*

TRICK OF THE TRADE

If your ex lies during her direct or cross examination, do not immediately refute her. Your attorney should politely restate her statement and ask her to repeat her lie <u>again</u>, digging a deeper hole for herself. Then he can destroy her credibility by cross examining her as to evidence exhibits that contradict her testimony. This is usually possible several times during a hearing if the attorney is well prepared.

CHAPTER **3** **A COMPLETE TEXT OF:**

FIGHTING FALSE ALLEGATIONS OF DOMESTIC VIOLENCE AND CHILD ABUSE

by

RONALD L. ISAACS, J.D.
ATTORNEY AT LAW

THE FATHERS' RIGHTS FOUNDATION
http://www.fathers-rights.com

Section One

The Truth About Domestic Violence

As militant feminists become more powerful and well funded, we see a dramatic increase in the use of false allegations of domestic violence and child abuse to gain an advantage in contested divorce and child custody cases.

Your local women's center depends on the filings of domestic abuse cases to justify their funding from the public and government agencies. The more women who go through women's centers who allege they were battered, the more monetary support the centers will receive. Permanent paid staffs are now on the payroll with a vested interest in generating complaints of domestic abuse. Huge government subsidies have created a bureaucracy employing many feminists. One local women's center boasts a $750,000 yearly budget, mostly from government grants and mostly paid out to a staff dedicated to punishing men just because they are men. The presence of vulnerable women and children at the centers often attracts eager lesbian volunteers. Now, thanks to the Domestic Violence Against Women (not men) Act, your tax dollars pay salaries for full time employees at your local courthouse.Their only function is to help "victims"(if they are women). Local prosecutors aggressively prosecute men solely on the word of a woman while refusing to prosecute women out of fear of the militant feminist voting bloc. Mandatory arrest policies require police to arrest someone anytime they go out on a domestic dispute call. This always results in the man being arrested, regardless of who instigated the violence. This practice is common despite a special report issued by the U. S. Department of Justice in 1994, whose findings showed a third of the family murders involved a female as the killer. In spousal murders, women represented 41 percent of the killers. In murders of offspring, the figure rose to 55 percent. In situations involving children, the ratio of sons over daughters killed stood at 64 percent to 36. These statistics tell us we should be taking a hard look at the sexist nature of the way domestic violence is depicted and handled by the police.

Christine Hoff Sommers, in her book entitled *Who Stole Feminism?* (1994), cites statistics claiming that of all women who have committed cases of domestic violence, between one third and one half are repeat offenders.

A 1997 study by the Department of Psychology, California State University, to assess gender stereotyping found that "the prevalences of physical domestic violence for men and women are high and they are not statistically different in this population".

Women's centers help propagate misleading myths that all abusers are male, help women prepare fill-in-the-blank court documents, and often encourage women to exaggerate claims of abuse to obtain an ex-parte protective order against a husband. Most of these claims are presented to judges as emergency situations so that the husband is not present in court to defend himself. Without any hearing or any objective proof of danger to the woman, the man is deprived of his home, his property and access to his children!

The militant feminists have even succeeded in having laws passed that allow police to confiscate property (guns) from husbands who have a protective order issued against them. This is done even if the husband had no hearing before the protective order was issued! Clearly the taking of property from a person without him having any hearing violates the due process clause of the U.S. Constitution. This does not seem to worry weak-willed state legislators who are intimidated by militant feminists into passing outrageous legislation.

The Clinton Administration block-granted millions of dollars (Responsible Fatherhood Project, DHHS and The Domestic Violence Against Women Act), to women's centers and state's attorneys' offices to encourage filing of <u>criminal</u> battery cases against husbands. This encourages state's attorneys to file criminal battery charges based <u>solely</u> on the word of a woman, even without <u>any</u> evidence of physical harm. The more men are charged, the more grant money the state's attorneys and women's centers receive! At the same time the husband is criminally charged, he is hit with the ex-parte civil protective order that deprives him of access to his children or property. The criminal legal system is aiding women in gaining the upper hand in custody battles. The system ignores that women are mentally abusing their children through denial of time and relationships with their fathers. Children cry out in loneliness caused by malicious, misguided and greedy individuals.

The ante has been raised. Now, husbands wishing to fight for custody face false, cruel and criminal claims that sometimes even include false claims of child sexual abuse. This greatly increases the husband's legal expenses and reduces his funds available to fight for custody.

Often the husband is tricked into pleading guilty to domestic violence in exchange for a small fine. He thinks he is avoiding spending all of his funds on a criminal defense. In reality he has just about ruined his custody case. He is now an admitted abuser. His ex knows she holds the power over him to get him arrested anytime. Some states mandate that a second offense is mandatory jail time! Of course, throughout this, the woman incurs <u>no</u> legal expense to obtain her protective order and the husband's own tax dollars are paying the salary of the State's Attorney prosecuting his wife's false claims! The following chapters tell how to protect against such tactics.

Section Two

Deceptive Practices Taught by Women Centers

The Ex-Parte Protective Order:

Your spouse, ex-spouse or live-in partner can obtain an order stripping you of your constitutional rights without you even knowing that she is appearing before a judge! She simply alleges that you would be a danger to her if you knew she was asking for the order!

The order can render you homeless and childless, without so much as your toothbrush or any right to see your children. It may take several days or weeks until a hearing is scheduled to determine whether the order will be made permanent. A woman need not show any evidence of physical abuse and can often obtain these emergency orders based solely on allegations of mental abuse!

Women's centers and courthouses keep fill-in- the-blank forms on file and encourage women to file them. Often feminists coach women into exaggerating the claim of abuse and using "hot button" words to make sure the judge will react and sign the order without any objective proof.

Most states require that you be allowed visitation in the order, but that provision is seldom included as the woman commonly alleges that because she was "abused," the children may be endangered (a real stretch of logic). Women use this as a ploy to get the upper hand in contested custody cases, forcing fathers to agree to outrageous demands for property or custody rights just so the lonely father can see his children.

You will have to hire a lawyer to defend you against the outrageous order. If the order contains provable false allegations, you should petition for your attorney fees and for sanctions against the filing party and her attorney or women's center's advisor/assistant. You should also use the false allegations and requests to deny access to children as evidence that the mother is willing to engage in mental child abuse to gain an advantage in a custody action. Filing a false pleading is always actionable against the filer and her attorney if she knew the allegations were false or made no attempt to determine the truth or falsity of the allegations.

Your rights to your children have been ruled as fundamental rights by the US Supreme Court (see App 9). No one may restrict access to your child absent evidence that you are a present serious danger to the child. You need never negotiate away these rights. Ultimately, they will be protected by the court. In some states, interfering with visitation is a criminal offense.

Section Three
The Criminalizing of Divorce

The Clinton Administration pushed the use of the Domestic Violence Against Women Act and subsidized women's centers and state's attorneys with millions of dollars to encourage criminal prosecutions for Domestic Violence (against women). Women are being encouraged to file criminal domestic battery charges immediately after filing for a protective order and file for divorce at the same time.

Based <u>solely</u> on your wife's word, with <u>no</u> corroborating evidence, local State's Attorneys are filing criminal charges against accused husbands for violating a civil order of protection! The prosecutors know that if the accused pleads not guilty and demands a jury trial the charge will eventually be dropped for lack of evidence. They participate in this added harassment of men for the sake of political correctness and to collect government grant money. Of course this means men incur legal fees (often $5,000) for defense in criminal actions while the women do not have to pay the State's Attorney for helping them gain an advantage in the woman's custody action.

In one recent case a police officer responded to a call only to find a wife who had obtained an ex-parte protective order for alleged mental abuse by her disabled husband who was so weak that he required constant oxygen usage. The disabled man's bedridden elderly mother lived with the couple in a home the man owned before he was remarried. The officer refused to force the man and his mother from his home. The officer was censured by his department because he violated the mandatory arrest policy of the police department. The husband and his elderly mother were forced to leave until he found an attorney who forced an expeditious hearing to vacate the bogus protective order several days later. He, in fact, was lucky. Most officers would have arrested him simply for being in his own house against the provisions of a protective order obtained without his knowledge.

Section Four
Steps to Protect and Defend Yourself

The following steps are recommended if you are served with a protective order or arrested for violating an order:

1. **Fight the Protective Order.** App. 1 in the appendix is a sample Motion to Open the Order (have it dismissed) and for Sanctions for False Pleadings.

2. **Fight the criminal case**. Without having an attorney make your initial appearance, plead not guilty and demand a jury trial and request time to find an attorney. No prosecutor wants the trouble and expense for a jury trial on such a minor matter. Then serve a Discovery Request on the State's Attorney (App. 3 in the Appendix) and hire a lawyer if the State's Attorney is not willing to drop the case. The case now suddenly looks like trouble instead of the normal rollover for a $25.00 fine he was expecting.

   Do not plea bargain. It will be used against you in your custody case as an admission that you are an abuser. A second offense sometimes means mandatory jail time. If you plead guilty
   to a first offense for a small fine, your ex has you over a barrel and knows she can make another false allegation any time she wants to pull your chain.

3. **Delay the criminal proceedings until <u>after</u> the divorce or custody proceedings are complete**. A Motion to Continue (App. 4) is in the appendix.

4. If you are interviewed or arrested for any reason, **especially child abuse**, make **<u>no</u>** statement. **<u>Nothing</u>. <u>Nada</u>.** Call your attorney and ask to be released on your own recognizance (no money down). When you ask to call your attorney all questions must cease.

5. **If arrested, request to file a countercharge and a charge for filing a false police report.** Make sure there is a record made of your demand. If you can be arrested <u>solely</u> on a woman's word, she should also be subject to arrest <u>solely</u> on your word. Try it. You'll be amazed at the double standard, but you must make a record!

TRICK OF THE TRADE

If arrested, request to file a countercharge and a charge for filing a false police report. Make sure there is a record made of your demand. If you can be arrested <u>solely</u> on a woman's word, she should also be subject to arrest <u>solely</u> on your word. Try it. You'll be amazed at the double standard, but you must *make a record!*

Section Five
Making the False Allegations Backfire

Do not plead guilty to any criminal action or admit abusing your wife. You can turn her accusation against her by alleging she is filing false claims to deny you visitation and time with your kids. Even if you did abuse your wife, what has that to do with how you treat your children?

Duty to Facilitate - Most courts require a custodial parent to affirmatively facilitate the relationship between the non-custodial parent and the children. Being unable or unwilling to facilitate that relationship may disqualify a person from custody. Obviously, filing a protective order that keeps you from your children is the best evidence of not being willing to facilitate that relationship.

Recent case law declares a duty of the custodial parent to foster the relationship between the non- custodial parent or face a change of custody:

> "The trial court should enforce this obligation (duty to facilitate) by explicitly telling the custodial parent about it and further informing the custodial parent that if he or she is unwilling or unable to meet it, then the **court stands fully prepared to change the custody** order and grant custody of the children to the non custodial parent to see if that parent could do a better job of meeting this obligation." **<u>In re Dobey</u> 629 N E 2d 812 (Feb. 1994)**

Your spouse's false allegations (made to interfere with your access to the children) are your **<u>best evidence</u>** that she cannot, or will not, facilitate the relationship between you and your children. Her conduct is, in fact, **<u>mental abuse of the children.</u>** Thus, she is unfit for custody. **She is a child abuser!** She is willing to cause heartache and emotional damage to the children so she can gain an advantage in negotiating a settlement with you. This is a basis for your requesting temporary custody pending the outcome of litigation and this is the argument you must strenuously make to the Judge.

A TRICK OF THE TRADE

If you argue that your spouse is unfit because her own pleadings and actions try to minimize vice maximize your time with the children while your pleadings ask for maximum involvement of **both** parents, you place your spouse in a legal box. She will either increase her offers or look foolish trying to explain to a cross-examiner why she should have more time with the children than you. She would run a serious risk of losing or not obtaining custody. Either way you better your position and minimize emotional damage to the children. Even if you don't win custody, you will enjoy much more visitation than fathers usually are awarded. Other tactics and a cross examination to use are in the *Multi-State Guide to Fathers' Rights* available from this publisher or on the internet at http://www.fathers-rights.com.

Section Six

Discovery as a Defense

You have the right under court procedural rules to know everything that will be presented at any hearing. The process to find out all that your opponent knows and prevent any surprise at hearings is called discovery. Use the discovery process to its fullest extent. To not use it is malpractice and a sure way to lose.

A) Take depositions. A deposition is a witness testimony under oath, in front of a court reporter, taken well before any court hearing. This pins down any accusations so they don't keep growing during the course of litigation. An accusing party should be deposed very quickly. Otherwise, she will change her story as necessary.

Often family members and friends will get together and all make false allegations. When they are deposed, they will be prepared to answer your questions about what they know, heard, etc. They will not be prepared to answer questions about what the other accusers have told them as to what the others saw, when they saw it, etc. Often their stories will contradict the other accuser's version of the facts. If an accuser says abuse occurred in the bedroom and her friend testifies the accuser told her it was in the kitchen, you have reasonable doubt as to the truthfulness of the bedroom abuse allegation!

Through discovery, find out every person the accuser talked to after the alleged abuse. Obtain copies of all written statements by subpoena if necessary. Different versions may have been told to each witness.

You will often discover a pattern of escalating accusations over a period of days. One recent accusation of sexual harassment escalated from being "brushed against" as told to witness A, to having her "butt patted" to next witness B, to being groped on the buttocks as told to police and recorded in the official police report. Of course finding each of these witnesses and interviewing them led to a defeat of the false allegations. In another case, one witness stated that Z told her she was assaulted in the bedroom and the next witness stated that Z told her she was assaulted in the kitchen! Proving the accuser is exaggerating her accusations will result in her total loss of credibility and cast doubt on the truthfulness of any statement she makes in subsequent hearings, even on unrelated matters.

B) In any case, serve written interrogatories (questions) and Requests to Produce Documents on your opponents. Sample Interrogatories and Requests to Produce are part of the *Case Organizer* offered by the author on the internet but are too lengthy to reproduce in this format. These should be completed before the deposition so you may ask clarifying questions.

Section Seven
Attack, Attack, Attack!

If you have been served with a protective order and/or arrested, you must attack back legally. **You cannot simply defend.** Some people will not pay any attention to you until you put their career, house and car on the line.

1. **Petition for custody based on the filing of false allegations.** Filing allegations that intentionally cause separation of the children from you is mental abuse of the children. If your wife is smart, she will give you all the visitation you want while litigation is pending. If she is not, she risks losing custody. Most custody cases that are won by fathers now are won because the mother interfered with visitation. If your spouse has filed papers requesting that you only receive every other weekend or limited visitation, those pleadings support your argument that her false allegations were also meant to intentionally deprive you of access to your children.

2. **Petition for Sanctions and attorney fees** against any person who helped prepare any false allegations in court documents .

3. Sue police officers and prosecutors in FEDERAL Court if they infringed on your civil rights and rights of due process under the Civil Rights Act and Section 1983.

4. Sue women's centers if they participated in exaggerating allegations or hid the children from you when there was no court order depriving you of custody. Until there is such an order, no one, not even the police, may keep your children from you. A mother has **NO** superior right over a father as to custody of children.

5. File kidnaping charges with the FBI against **anyone** who secretes your children from you. There have actually been prison sentences imposed on women's center employees who attempted to conceal a child from a father who had custody. An underground organization coordinated by feminists is said to be active in concealing children from fathers

6. **Go to your local newspaper and tell your story.** Sometimes this will prevent further abuses of the legal system by feminists supported by weak-willed public officials. If you can not get a story written, write a letter to the editor for publishing.

7. **Attack the funding of centers that violate basic constitutional rights.** Contact their sponsors and object to any community funds that subsidize centers that promote false accusations and break up families.

CHAPTER 4 DENIAL OF VISITATION PROBLEMS

In January 1994, denial of court-ordered visitation was deemed a **criminal offense** in Illinois. **See: 720 ILCS 5/10-5.5(b).**

> "Every person who, in violation of the visitation provisions of a court order relating to child custody, detains or conceals a child with the intent to deprive another person of his or her rights to visitation shall be guilty of unlawful visitation interference." 720 ILCS 5/10-5.5(b).

The importance of obtaining **specifically detailed visitation orders** cannot be stressed enough. If your order does not have **specific** holidays, days, dates, times and locations for exchange of the children, a peace officer cannot and will not enforce your visitation rights.

TRICK OF THE TRADE

*Read about your **fundamental Constitutional** right to parent in Lulay v. Lulay on the last pages of this book. Use those arguments in your filings and court hearings!*

WHAT IS REASONABLE VISITATION?

The Supreme Court of Illinois defined reasonable visitation as follows:
A reasonable visitation schedule is one that will preserve and foster the child's relationship with the non custodial parent. In re Marriage of Eckert, 119 IL. 2d 316, 327 (1988).

Reasonable visitation is 50/50 visitation. **Every other weekend and holiday and short vacations cannot by anyone's definition be called maximum involvement!**

TRICK OF THE TRADE

Show a judge a poster size calender with only that typical visitation schedule colored in and he will immediately begin to add more days to balance out visitation!

DOES VISITATION CAUSE LACK OF STABILITY?

Mothers opposing visitation often argue that extensive visitation cannot provide the needed stability for the child and that "shuttling the child back and forth is unsettling." Simply stated, however:

> "While single-custody may be characterized by physical stability and continuity, the child's emotional well-being may not be enhanced by it. No evidence supports the argument that it is harmful to let a child live with both parents. It is apparent that the 'stability' which is important is not physical stability but rather emotional stability. Emotional stability is a function of the child's sense of security. If the child knows that he or she is wanted by and can live with both parents, the child's sense of security will be enhanced." Bratt, Joint Custody, 67 Kentucky L. Rev. 271 at 298 (1978-79); see also Steinman, The Experience of Children in a Joint-Custody Arrangement, 51 Am. J. Orthopsychiatry 403 (1981). Of children studied, only 25 percent experienced confusion and anxiety about their schedules and switching houses.

TRICK OF THE TRADE

*Don't forget the **COMMON SENSE** argument that the child is probably already being switched back and forth to day care and babysitters and church nurseries. Surely being placed with the father is less unsettling to the child than these everyday transfers! When overnight visits are discussed, talk about reading your children bedtime stories and the children running to your bedroom in a storm and children being sick at night and how you need to be there for them during the night also to maintain your relationship with the children. Maximum possible visitation or joint custody recognizes the child's rights to a continuing and extensive relationship with both parents while giving the greatest **EMOTIONAL STABILITY** to the children of divorce. This is your counter argument.*

CAN THE EX-WIFE DENY REASONABLE VISITATION?

Illinois statutes and most state laws presume that maximum involvement with both parents is in the best interests of the child. It places the burden of proof on the party opposing maximum involvement. The following cases require the person opposing maximum involvement to prove her case.

> "In Illinois, it appears that the party against whom an evidentiary presumption operates is required to carry the burden of going forward with some opposing evidence. The required amount or weight of such evidence necessary to rebut the presumption is determined by the strength of the presumption." See Franciscan Sisters Health Care v. Dean, 95 Ill. 2d 452, 69 Ill. Dec. 960, 448 N.E. 2d 872 (1983); In re Marriage of Rosen, 126 Ill. App. 3d 766, 81 Ill. Dec. 840, 467 N.E. 2d 962 (1st Dist. 1984); Corkery Outline of Marital and Non-Marital Property Law in Illinois, 1985 Ill. Fam. L. Rep.158, 160 (Aug. 1985).

CAN THE EX CONTROL YOUR VISITATION?

Your spouse has **no** right to control your visitation location or activities and even a court cannot interfere with or restrict your plans unless the children are **endangered.**

> "A parent not granted custody of the child is entitled to reasonable visitation rights unless the Court finds, after a hearing, that visitation would **endanger seriously the child's physical, mental, moral, or emotional health."** 750 ILCS 6/607(a)

With respect to the restriction of visitation, **the endangerment standard is an onerous one** (In re Marriage of Hanson (1983), 112 Ill. App. 3d 564, 568; In re Marriage of Neat (1981), 101 Ill. App. 3d 1046, 1048), **and is more stringent or exacting than the best-interest standard** (In re Marriage of Solomon (1980), 84 Ill. App. 3d 901, 907; Ill. Ann. Stat., ch. 40, par. 607(c), Supplement to Historical and Practice Notes, at 27 (Smith-Hurd Supp. 1983); see In re Marriage of Neat (1981), 101 Ill. App. 3d 1046, 1048). **Where the custodial parent seeks to restrict visitation rights, he or she bears the burden of proving by a preponderance of the evidence that the existing visitation seriously endangers the child.** (Griffiths v. Griffiths (1984), 127 Ill. App. 3d 126, 129; In re Marriage of Neat (1981), 101 Ill. App. 3d 1046, 1048.) In re Marriage of Anderson, 474 N.E.2d 911, 130 Ill. App. 3d 684 (1985).

A restriction on visitation is action which limits, restrains, or confines visitation within bounds. (In Re Marriage of Tisckos/ Stewart (1987), 161 Ill. App. 3d 302, 310,514 N.E.2d 523, 528.) A termination of visitation is a restriction (In re Marriage of Dunn (1987), 155 Ill. App. 3d 247, 254, 508 N.E.2d 250, 255), as is **a prohibition on overnight visitation. Likewise, a requirement that visitation be supervised, occur in the home of the custodial parent, or outside the home of the noncustodial parent is a restriction.** (Tisckos/Stewart, 161 Ill. App. 3d at 310, 514 N.E.2d at 528). In re the Marriage LaTour, 608 N.E.2d 1339, 241 Ill. App. 3d 500, (1993).

In other words, if the child is not endangered, what happens during your visitation or where you go to enjoy it is no business of your ex or the court.

A FATHER'S RIGHT TO BABYSIT

Many times an ex- wife is so spiteful that she would rather pay a babysitter than allow a dad more time with his children. Sometimes this backfires and can be used as evidence of the lack of fitness of the ex for custody. After all, isn't this mental child abuse -- denying a child time with his/her father?

The custodial parent placing the child with a third party rather than allowing the other parent the opportunity for additional visitation is engaging in an unreasonable denial of visitation.

> **"The custodial parent has the duty to strengthen and nurture in every way possible to relationship between the children and the non-custodial parent....** By allowing the father to serve as his child's babysitter when he is available the father can still be a significant part of the child's life even though he doesn't have custody . . . **We fail to see how one could reasonably argue that the child's best interests are better served by having a babysitter care for him instead of his father.** In Re Dobey, 629 N E 2d 812, 196 Ill. Dec. 267 (1994).

TRICK OF THE TRADE

Another point to raise is that if the mother has money to spend on babysitters when the children could have been with their father, she is wasting the children's child support money and child support should be reduced so the father can spend the money on the children during his visitation periods.

TRICK OF THE TRADE

When weekday visits are limited to a few hours argue that it ***<u>does</u>*** *make a difference where the children sleep, who reads them bedtime stories, whose room they run to during a storm, who treats nighttime illnesses. USE EMOTION!*

DUTY OF MOTHER TO FACILITATE FATHER'S RELATIONSHIP WITH CHILD

Recent case law declares a duty of the custodial parent to **foster (not just tolerate)** the relationship between the non-custodial parent and the child or face a change of custody:

> "The trial court should enforce this obligation by explicitly telling the custodial parent about it and further informing the custodial parent that if he or she is unwilling or unable to meet it, then the court stands **fully prepared to change the custody order** and grant custody of the children to the non-custodial parent to see if that parent could do a better job of meeting this obligation." In re Dobey 629 N E 2d 812 (Feb. 1994).

TRICK OF THE TRADE

Many times a mother will deny visitation to exert pressure on a father to pay more support or to gain a more favorable division of property in a divorce action. ***This is the best thing she can do to aid a father's attempt to gain custody!*** *Documentation of denials of visitation is necessary. Calenders and diaries recording attempts to gain visitation are necessary. Eyewitness testimony of unrelated parties greatly bolster a father's case.*

TRICK OF THE TRADE

Prepare a 4'x4' calendar showing every day of the past 12 months. Put a red dot on every day you didn't have visitation and a green dot on days you did. This makes the visitation history easy for the judge to understand. I have often seen judges say, "Let's put some green here and here and here to balance out the colors." If you only enjoy every other weekend visitation you will be amazed at how this looks on a yearly calendar. Vinyl calenders and colored stick on dots are available at office supply businesses.

CHAPTER 5 CAN THE EX-WIFE MOVE AWAY?

In today's mobile society you may very likely face the prospect of your ex moving away with your children. However, more courts are requiring the move to be in the child's, not the parent's, best interest. If your state defines best interest as maximum involvement, the removal of a child, reducing visitation, would be "per se" not in the child's best interest. **Protect yourself by putting a distance restriction in any marriage settlement agreement.** If your ex is successful in moving away, the judge will usually make her pay all travel expenses and give you all school vacation time as visitation, although this is unacceptable!

TRICK OF THE TRADE

If the move is to benefit a new spouse's career, it should be argued that the new husband benefitting from the move knowingly married into an existing family and he should be the one to bear the burden of commuting, not you or the kids!

The deficit of the child losing close contact with the non-custodial parent must be offset and outweighed by other significant advantages in the child' s --***not the custodial parent's***-- best interest. Cases addressing moving a child out of state often address maximum involvement:

> "Moreover, a trial court's examination of a removal petition should be guided by the policy of the Illinois Marriage and Dissolution of Marriage Act in custody matters, which states, inter alia, that the **purpose of the Act is to "secure the maximum involvement and cooperation of both parents** regarding the physical, mental, moral, and emotional well-being of the children during and after litigation". In re Marriage of Eckert, 119 IL. 2d 316, 328 (1988).

TRICK OF THE TRADE

The LAST question to ask a mother seeking removal: "You are aware that your ex husband is asking for custody. If you lose your motion to remove, will you stay here or leave the child behind and still move?" (Either answer will kill her case for removal) If she would stay you can then argue she has agreed to stay even if the hubby leaves. If she says she will leave the child behind she loses custody for sure.

PARENTAL RIGHTS ARE PROTECTED BY FEDERAL CASE LAW

The cases cited below interpret the **U.S. Constitution** as protecting a parent's rights and define those rights as **fundamental** rights, **the most protected of all rights**.

See Lulay v. Lulay on last pages of this book also See, e.g., Meyer v. Nebraska, 262 U.S. 390, 67 L. ed. 1042, 43 S. Ct. 625 (1923); Pierce vs. Society of Sisters, 268 U.S. 510, 69 L. Ed. 1070, 45 S. Ct. 571 (1925); Stanley v. Illinois, 405 U.S. 645, 31 L. Ed. 2d 551, 92 S. Ct. 1208 (1972); Wisconsin v. Yoder, 406 U.S. 205, 32 L. Ed. 2d 15, 92 S. Ct. 1526 (1972); Moore v. City of East Cleveland, 431 U.S. 494, 52 L. Ed. 2d 531, 97 S. Ct. 1932 (1977); Smith v. Organization of Foster Families, 431 U.S. 816; 53 L. Ed. 2d 14, 97 S. Ct. 2094 (1977); Santosky v. Kramer, 455 U.S. 745, 71 L. Ed. 2d 599, 102 S. Ct. 1388 (1982).

Fundamental rights may not be restricted by state action if there is a **less restrictive alternative** available to accomplish public policy. See Shelton vs. Tucker, 364 U.S. 4798, 488, 5 L. Ed. 2d 231, 81 S.Ct. 247 (1960).

This basic legal concept would give even an abusing father a right to supervised visitation. However, a supervision requirement on a father **who does not represent a danger to his child's mental or physical health would be an unconstitutional restriction on his parental rights** since there is a less restrictive method of granting visitation and a requirement for supervision would not further any legitimate purpose of the state.

Rights to reasonable visitation are **NOT NEGOTIABLE**. Do not fear, you will get at least your visitation rights, if not custody, if you persevere, regardless of what your ex or her lawyer or the women's center wants or thinks.

CHAPTER 6 STATE LAWS PROTECT PARENTAL RIGHTS

All states recognize and protect parental rights:

> "Therefore such **rights** which are shared equally during marriage **must remain as much as possible undiminished by divorce."** See: Ill. Rev. Stat. 755 ILCS 5/11-7

Illinois law, 750 ILCS 5/602.1 states:

> (a) The dissolution of marriage, the declaration of invalidity of marriage, the legal separation of the parents, or the parents' living separate and apart **shall not diminish parental powers, rights**, and responsibilities except as the Court for good reason may determine under standards of Section 602 (Best Interest-Maximum Involvement tests).

LESS THAN MAXIMUM INVOLVEMENT WITH YOUR CHILD IS A DIMINISHMENT OF YOUR PARENTAL RIGHTS *AS WELL AS PRESUMPTIVELY* ***NOT*** *IN THE CHILD'S BEST INTEREST! THESE RIGHTS ARE* ***NON-NEGOTIABLE !***

Following is a general discussion of Missouri law which is fairly typical:

CHILD CUSTODY

1. Subject Matter Jurisdiction for Initial Order of Custody

A. Jurisdictional Grounds

The Missouri Uniform Child Custody Jurisdiction Act is applicable to initial orders of custody. To have jurisdiction, the court must find one of the following:

1) Home State

Missouri will have jurisdiction if Missouri is the child's home state. A home state is defined as the state in which the child has resided for six consecutive months immediately preceding the commencement of the litigation;

2) Extended Home State

Missouri was the home state within 6 months before commencement of the proceeding, and while the child is no longer present in the state one of the parents continues to live in Missouri;

3) Significant Connection

The child and at least one litigant have a significant connection with the state and evidence concerning the child is available in the state;

4) Emergencies

The child is present within the state and has been abandoned or is subject to abuse or neglect;

5) No Other State Has Jurisdiction

No other state has appropriate jurisdiction or another state has declined jurisdiction in favor of this state.

B. Concurrent Jurisdiction

If two states have a right to assume jurisdiction under their versions of the UCCJA, then the state where the petition was first filed shall have jurisdiction to decide the question of custody and the sister state shall defer jurisdiction.

C. Unclean Hands

Even if a state has jurisdiction under the UCCJA, it can decline jurisdiction if the party seeking to invoke custody jurisdiction has engaged in wrongful conduct.

2. Personal Jurisdiction in Custody Awards

If both parents are present or if one is a non-resident but subject to the matrimonial long arm statute, then the court has in personam jurisdiction to enter a custody order. If one or both of the parents are not present in the state nor subject to long arm jurisdiction, then the court may assume quasi in rem jurisdiction to decide custody. Custody, like marriage, is a status that the court has power over so long as the child is present in the state.

3. Procedures in a Custody Case

A. Priority

Custody proceedings are to receive a priority setting within the courts.

B. Guardian Ad Litem

In all contested cases, the court may appoint a guardian ad litem for the child. If there have been any allegations of abuse or neglect, then the court is required to appoint a guardian ad litem.

C. Home Study

The court may order an investigator to prepare a report concerning the child. The report must be furnished to the parties or counsel at least ten days prior to the hearing but cannot be presented to the judge prior to the hearing.

D. In Chambers Interview

The judge is permitted to interview the children involved in the dispute in chambers. Counsel for both parties have a right to be present and a record of the interview must be made.

E. Hearsay Testimony

The court may permit hearsay testimony in a child custody case if it concludes that it would not be in the best interest of the child to be required to give testimony in open court.

F. Waiver of Evidentiary Privileges

If there are allegations of abuse or neglect and custody is contested, any party seeking custody waives evidentiary privileges such as doctor-patient privileges.

4. Types of Child Custody Orders

There are three primary types of child custody orders:

A. Sole Custody

1) Definition

Sole custody occurs when only one of the parents is given physical custody and the right to decide matters involving the education, health, care and religious training of the child.

2) Obligation to Confer with the Non-Custodial Parent

Even though sole custody has been ordered, the court may require the sole custodian to confer with non-custodial parent before decisions are made. In the absence of this specific order, the sole custodian is not required to confer.

3) Access to Records

Unless visitation is denied, the non-custodial parent is entitled to all medical, dental, school records and information concerning the health, education, and welfare of the child.

B. Joint Custody

Joint custody might be legal and/or physical.

1) Joint Legal Custody
Joint legal custody means the sharing of decision making rights, responsibility and authority.

2) Joint Physical Custody
Joint physical custody means that each parent is awarded significant periods of time during which the child resides with him/her or is under his/her care and supervision.

3) Joint Custody Plan
A decree providing for joint custody must include a specific written plan setting forth the terms of custody.

C. Third Party Custody

Custody may be ordered to a third party if it is in the best interest of the child. There is, however, a presumption in favor of the biological parent that can be overcome by showing either:

1) Unfitness
The biological parent is unfit; or

2) Extraordinary Circumstances
Extraordinary circumstances have been found where a child has psychologically bonded with a third party such as a grandparent.

5. The Standard for Awarding Child Custody

A. Best Interest of the Child

1) Factors to be Considered to Determine the Best Interest of the Child

a) The wishes of the child's parent as to his custody;

b) The wishes of a child as to his custodian;

c) The interaction and interrelationship of the child with his parents, his siblings, and any other person who may significantly affect the child's best interest;

d) The child's adjustment to his home, school, and the community;

e) The mental and physical health of all individuals involved including any history of abuse of any individuals involved;

f) **The needs of the child for a continuing relationship with both parents** and the ability and willingness of parents to actively perform their functions as mother and father for the needs of the child;

g) The intention of either parent to relocate his or her residence outside the state; and

TRICK OF THE TRADE
(h) is YOUR WINNING ARGUMENT!!!!!!!!

h) ***Which parent is more likely to allow the child frequent and meaningful contact with the other parent.***

2) **Factors which <u>cannot</u> be considered in making an award in child custody:**

a) gender of the children;

b) age of the children;

c) financial status of the parties.

3) **Preference for Joint Custody**
It is the policy in Missouri to encourage substantial and meaningful contacts between the child and both parents subsequent to dissolution. This has been interpreted to mean that Missouri has a preference for joint custody to the extent that joint custody is in the best interest of the child.

(4 & 5 omitted)

6) **Visitation Rights**

There is an absolute right for a non-custodial parent to have reasonable visitation rights with their child **unless visitation will be harmful** to the physical or psychological well-being of the child.

7) **Grandparent Visitation Rights**

A. **Ninety Days Without Visitation**
If it is in the best interest of the child, the court may order grandparent visitation if it has been unreasonably denied for ninety days or more.

B. **Death of Parent**
If one parent is deceased and the surviving parent denies reasonable visitation rights to either the maternal or paternal grandparent, the court can order visitation if it is in the best interest of the child.

C. **Dissolution and Subsequent Adoption**
If one parent is deceased and the child is subsequently adopted and reasonable visitation has been denied a grandparent who was a legal grandparent prior to the adoption, the court may order visitation if it is in the best interest of the child.

<u>MODIFICATION OF CHILD CUSTODY</u>

1. **Jurisdiction to Modify**

A. **Original Order Entered in Missouri**
If the original custody order was entered in Missouri, then the court which entered the decree continues to have jurisdiction so long as one of the four grounds for jurisdiction under the UCCJA have been established. those grounds are:

1) **Home State**
Missouri is the home state of the child or was the home state within six months of the filing of the motion for modification;

2) **Significant Connection**
The child and at least one litigant have a significant connection with the state and evidence concerning the child is available in this state;

3) **Emergency**
The child is present within the state and has been abandoned or subject to abuse or neglect;

4) **No Other State to Assume Jurisdiction**
No other state has appropriate jurisdiction or another state has declined jurisdiction in favor of Missouri.

B. **Original Order Entered Outside of Missouri**
If Missouri did not enter the original order, then Missouri can modify only if:

1) **Missouri has Jurisdiction Under the UCCJA**
Missouri has jurisdiction under the UCCJA because it is the home state, there are significant connections, there is emergency jurisdiction, or no other state has jurisdiction; **AND**

2) **No Jurisdiction in Original Court**
The original court no longer has jurisdiction under its laws or has declined to exercise jurisdiction.

Example: The original custody decree was entered in Kansas, but the child and one parent subsequently moved to the state of Missouri where they lived for nine months prior to the filing of the motion for modification. Missouri is now the home state but it still does not have jurisdiction to modify the custody order. Kansas retains jurisdiction to modify because it continues to have a significant connection with the custody dispute because the child lived there for a substantial period of time and one of the parents continues to live there. If Kansas were to decline to exercise jurisdiction, then Missouri could modify the custody order. Otherwise, Missouri will not be able to obtain modification jurisdiction until there are no further ties between Kansas, the child and the non- custodial parent.

2. **Standard for Modification**

A. **Changed Circumstances Since the Original Decree**
Modification is permitted if circumstances of child or custodian have changed since entry of the custody order;

1) Changes in the circumstances of the <u>non-custodial</u> parent do not trigger re-examination of the custody question. Joint custodians are both considered custodians for purposes of this rule.

2) A breakdown in the joint custody agreement can be a circumstance justifying modification of the custody order.

B. **Facts Previously Not Considered**
Modification of child custody can also be justified by facts which were not considered by the court at the time of the entry of the initial custody decree.

Example: **If at the time of the custody hearing, the court was not notified that the custodial parent was alcoholic and abusive to the child, that information can be the basis for a modification action even though the evidence was in existence and have been brought to the court's attention in the first hearing.**

3. Removal from Missouri of a Child Subject to a Missouri Custody Order

A child who is the subject of a Missouri custody order cannot be removed from the state for more than ninety consecutive days without prior court approval or written agreement of the parties. Violation of this provision is sufficient evidence of a changed circumstance to permit reexamination of the question of who should have custody of the children.

ENFORCEMENT OF CHILD CUSTODY

1. Habeas Corpus
A writ of habeas corpus requires a party who is wrongfully holding the child from the legal custodian to produce the child.

2. Contempt of Court
The civil contempt powers of the court may be used to ensure that a child is returned to the custodial parent as required by the decree or to compel a custodial parent to allow court ordered visitation.

3. Criminal Sanctions

A. Knowing violation of a Custody Order
It is a crime for an individual who knows he has no legal right to do so to take or entice a child from the person who has been granted custody by a court order.

B. Post Dissolution Petition
It is a criminal violation if one removes the child from the custody of the parent who had custody at the time the petition for dissolution was filed.

4. Tort Liability for Interference with Custody
The common law recognizes a tort for the intentional interference with custody. Only a custodian is entitled to damages so it is inapplicable to enforce visitation rights.

5. Parental Kidnapping Prevention Act

A. Statutory Full Faith and Credit
The Parental Kidnapping Prevention Act is a federal statute which requires the courts to give full faith and credit. Its purpose is to stabilize custody orders by clearly defining which state has the right to enter a decree of modification. There is no constitutional full faith and credit given to custody orders because custody orders are always subject to modification.

B. Preference for Home State
The PKPA requires states to enforce a custody order of another state but only if the state entering the custody decree had home state jurisdiction, unless at the time the order is entered, there is NO state that qualified as the home state.

C. No Federal Question Jurisdiction
While the PKPA is a federal statute, the Supreme Court has held that there is no federal question jurisdiction in the federal court to enforce the PKPA. This means that its enforcement is left to the state.

*These notes are from materials presented at the Missouri Bar Review Course which was held at the University of Missouri in Columbia, Missouri in June and July of 1993 ,may have changed and are for illustrative purposes only.

CHAPTER 7 EVEN UNWED FATHERS HAVE RIGHTS!

The Illinois Parentage Act of 1984 Section 4 5/16 which determines rights of unwed parents incorporates the Illinois Marriage and Dissolution of Marriage Act best interest standards as to modification of Custody/visitation. The U.S. Supreme Court has also supported full custody and visitation rights for unwed fathers. In **Stanley v. Illinois**, 405 U.S. 645 (1972) the Supreme Court stated:

> **"The Illinois Parentage Act clearly gives unwed fathers the same custody and visitation rights as the father of a child born during a marriage and requires the same best interest standard used in marriage dissolutions be used in paternity actions."**

This U.S. Supreme Court decision is controlling in all states.

*****CAUTION*****

In some states unwed fathers must claim paternity or register as a putative father within a very short time after the child's birth or nine months after conception even if he didn't know the woman was pregnant! These are **unconstitutional statutes** fostered by the feminist lobby. Any support order is considered a custody order under an Illinois Statute. Signing a voluntary support order may delay your rights to gain custody. Even if no warning was given on the support order that it awards custody to the mother, the mother will argue custody cannot be changed within two years of the order! This statute is also unconstitutional (a denial of due process notice) and usually not upheld by a court.

> "If a judgment of parentage contains no explicit award of custody, the establishment of a support obligation or of visitation rights in one parent shall be considered a judgment granting custody to the other parent. If the parentage judgment contains no such provisions, custody shall be presumed to be with the mother; however, the presumption shall not apply if the father has had physical custody for at least 6 months prior to the date that the mother seeks to enforce custodial rights." § 750 ILCS 45/14(a)(2).

Beware that when a support order is issued it can be argued that it grants custody to the parent receiving support and it may be difficult to change custody for 2 years except for endangerment of the child! However an Illinois court has ruled such an order is not a final order and awarded the unwed father custody despite the support order:

> **Unmarried fathers have a substantial and cognizable interest in the custody and care of their children born out of wedlock. (In re Custody of Horbatenko (1988), 176 Ill. App. 3d 970, 973.) However, this interest is distinguishable from that of a separated or divorced father in that a father who was for at least a time married to his child's mother would have participated in raising the child during the period of marriage. (Horbatenko, 176 Ill. App. 3d at 973.) A putative father must show a substantial concern for the child before he {*835} has acquired standing to assert his interests; his conduct in establishing a significant relationship with the child and in providing for the child are factors to be considered by the court in determining the best interests of the child. (In re Custody of Bourey (1984), 127 Ill. App. 3d 530, 534.)**
> **The trial court's award of custody will not be disturbed on review unless it is contrary to the manifest weight of the evidence or it works manifest injustice. Bourey, 127 Ill. App. 3d at 533. In Re Shelly Upmann 558 NE2d 568, 200 Ill App 3rd 827(July 1990 Second Dist, IL.) [Custody awarded to unwed father]**

TRICK OF THE TRADE

Your real problem here is usually grandparents wanting to take over a child. They will LOSE unless they can show the father is a DANGER to the child.

Other states have similar unconstitutional laws (see the **Stanley** case above) that discriminate against an illegitimate child's right to be treated like any other child, i.e., to have a relationship with his natural father. **When challenged, these laws usually fall.** These laws are enacted by weak- willed legislators bowing to pressure from women's groups. Often State Bar Associations have committees that recommend legislation that is rubber stamped and passed by the legislature without real review. The family law committees of the Bars tend to be left to the control of female lawyers, most of whom are previously divorced militant feminists. Where fathers' rights groups are not involved with their legislators, you will see more and more abusive and anti-male laws being passed.

CHAPTER 8 SAMPLE CROSS EXAMINATION OF (EX)WIFE

You **must** have petitioned for custody asking that **BOTH** parents enjoy maximum time with the child to effectively use this cross examination.

QUESTION 1: What are you willing to do to facilitate the relationship between your husband and his child(ren)? (The above is a test for fitness for custody. Regardless of answer, proceed)

QUESTION 2: What visitation schedule do you think is a reasonable visitation schedule that would facilitate the relationship between your (ex)husband and his child?
(She will usually describe a"minimal" visitation schedule)

QUESTION 3: Are you saying that "every other weekend and every other holiday" is enough visitation to maintain the relationship between your (ex)husband and the child?

QUESTION 4: As you are aware, your ex has <u>also</u> filed for custody in this case. (PAUSE) Assuming <u>he</u> gets custody, what visitation schedule should <u>you</u> have?

QUESTION 5: Why is more visitation required for your "reasonable" visitation then is required for reasonable visitation for your (ex) Husband?

- or -

Since you have just stated that you would be satisfied with much less time (the same as what she said for husband if she is smart enough to figure out how to respond to **Question 3**) with your child than you now have, you don't really want sole custody then, do you?

QUESTION 6: A custodial parent must do the utmost to protect the child's best interests. How are you evidencing your concern for the child's best interest by denying her right to have maximum involvement with both parents? (Usually answers "I am not.")

QUESTION 7: Then you have no objection to the child spending the maximum time possible with <u>both parents</u>, do you?

Do you see the box she is put in? On YOUR examination you should say you would give her the maximum time possible and bend over backwards to see the child receives maximum time with **<u>both</u>** parents.

CHAPTER 9 ALIMONY

Alimony is an area where the women's movement shot itself in the foot. Their strident claims that women are equal to men in the workplace have resulted in women being held to a higher standard of self-support. Alimony is seldom awarded absent a long marriage where an elderly spouse has been out of the work force. When alimony (maintenance) is awarded, it is usually for a short period of time in which specific education or training is to be finished. Most states' and countries' statutes encourage property distribution rather than alimony because it results in a clean break between divorcing spouses. Louisiana bars alimony if the spouse was adulterous. The Illinois statute is put forth below as an example of what courts consider in awarding maintenance.

> " Maintenance. (a) In a proceeding for dissolution of marriage or legal separation or declaration of invalidity of marriage, or a proceeding for maintenance following dissolution of the marriage by a court which lacked personal jurisdiction over the absent spouse, the court may grant a temporary or permanent maintenance award for either spouse in amounts and for periods of time as the court deems just, without regard to marital misconduct, in gross or for fixed or indefinite periods of time, and the maintenance may be paid from the income or property of the other spouse after consideration of all relevant factors, including:
> (1) the income and property of each party, including marital property apportioned and non-marital property assigned to the party seeking maintenance;
> (2) the needs of each party;
> (3) the present and future earning capacity of each party;
> (4) any impairment of the present and future earning capacity of the party seeking maintenance due to that party devoting time to domestic duties or having foregone or delayed education, training, employment, or career opportunities due to the marriage;
> (5) the time necessary to enable the party seeking maintenance to acquire appropriate education, training, and employment, and whether that party is able to support himself or herself through appropriate employment or is the custodian of a child making it appropriate that the custodian not seek employment;
> (6) the standard of living established during the marriage;
> (7) the duration of the marriage;
> (8) the age and the physical and emotional condition of both parties;
> (9) the tax consequences of the property division upon the respective economic circumstances of the parties;
> (10) contributions and services by the party seeking maintenance to the education, training, career or career potential, or license of the other spouse;
> (11) any valid agreement of the parties; and
> (12) any other factor that the court expressly finds to be just and equitable." 750 ILCS 5/504

Either spouse may be required to provide necessities for the other in the form of maintenance. **Don't overlook your right to ask for maintenance from your ex-wife especially when she is asking maintenance from you!**

CHAPTER 11 A complete text of:

HOW TO MINIMIZE CHILD SUPPORT

by

RONALD L. ISAACS, J.D.

Attorney at Law

HOW TO MINIMIZE CHILD SUPPORT

by Ronald L. Isaacs

TRUE HORROR STORIES

James has never been to Pennsylvania; he is served a summons to appear in his local county court. The local State's Attorney is pursuing an order to collect child support from James based on a Pennsylvania order saying they have determined he owes his ex-wife thousands of dollars of child support based on a hearing in Pennsylvania that James knew nothing about!

John has always paid his child support on time. His ex is not on welfare and makes $32,000 a year. John is served with a summons to appear from the local State's Attorney. He is advised that he is one of several "randomly picked" fathers whom the state is pursuing to increase child support, even though no welfare is being paid to his ex-wife. The State's Attorney only has legal authority to represent women who are receiving state aid, but asserts that since they are representing the ex for free, she is receiving state aid, so they can represent her under their new guidelines! CATCH 22!! Evidently, the government is pursuing fathers who are *already* paying their child support because it is easier to collect from them than from deadbeat dads!

STATISTICS

The U.S. Census Bureau has reported that fathers with joint custody pay 90.2% of all child support ordered; fathers with limited visitation rights pay 79.1%; and 44.5% of those fathers with NO visitation rights still financially support their children.

30% of custodial mothers not receiving child support have never asked for or do not want child support.

25% of custodial mothers do not receive child support because the father is unable to pay.

20 % of custodial mothers not receiving child support have made other financial arrangements with the father.

11% of custodial mothers not receiving child support do not have a child support order.

Of ten million custodial mothers only 7% (one out of fourteen) do not receive child support because of a deadbeat dad.

TABLE OF CONTENTS

WASTE OF CHILD SUPPORT MONEY

No one denies that a father has a duty to support his children. However, laws pushed onto timid legislators by militant feminists have created an atmosphere of coercion requiring the father to pay child support without any requirement for the mother to account for how the child support money is spent and without protecting the father's visitation rights.

If the legislators continue to refuse to provide accountability for spending of child support money or to enforce visitation rights, there is no alternative left to fathers except to minimize or avoid (to the extent legally possible) payment of unreasonable child support.

By keeping the ordered child support paid to an ex-spouse to a minimum, the paying spouse can make direct purchases of food, clothing and services for his children, and for his children alone. This is currently the only way fathers can be sure their money is being spent on their children.

Drug abuse is a growing phenomenon among single parents. Increasing amounts of child support money are being spent on drugs while children go hungry. This problem will only worsen until legislators step in to protect the children from wasting of child support.

Often, child support pays payments on an extravagant house or cars, yet the children own no equity in the property purchased with child support money. This must be changed! If child support is paying for property, the children's names should be on the deed to the house or title to the car!

Child support money is often used to pay lawyers for litigation to reduce the father's visitation or involvement with his child. The child's money is being spent to adversely affect the child's best interests, which is usually defined to be the maximum involvement of *both* parents in the child's life. Judges should be ever alert for this abuse and waste of children's assets.

The solution to these problems is legal consistency. Current law states that when a guardian for a mentally incompetent person is appointed, that guardian must file a yearly report with the Court detailing how every dime is spent and extraordinary expenses must be approved *before* the money is spent. The money is held in *trust* for the disabled person. Child support should also be considered held in trust for use **only** to benefit the children, **not** the ex- spouse. A regular accounting to a court of money spent is a reasonable method of protecting children's welfare.

Since it is unlikely that legislators will have the guts to stand up to the organized militant feminists, it is incumbent on the person paying support to **minimize** the money he must pay directly to the ex. This book will explore ways to minimize these payments.

LOWERING YOUR INCOME

All child support awards are based on income. Some states start with gross, some with net after taxes and allowed adjustments. The best way to lower your child support is to lower your income by one or more of the following methods:

a) **Income shifting.**

1. If you are a commission salesman, ask your boss if your wife could have a sales contract and help with sales. This opens many opportunities and possibilities to shift income to a spouse who actually participates in the sale. 2. If you are self-employed, consider putting your kids on the payroll for odd jobs or your new spouse as a manager. Pay your spouse well, the same as you would have to pay any other employee. The salaries paid lower your net income and thus, child support!

b) **Let your spouse do the saving**

Spend **your** income and let your new spouse save hers and put the earned interest into her separate bank accounts. In some states, this won't work unless you have a pre-nuptial agreement signed before your marriage!

c) **Rent from your spouse**

Consider renting your home office space, shop, vehicles or equipment from your new spouse or your parents. This gives you the additional benefit that rental income is not subject to social security taxes, saving about 20% of your earnings and, of course, you can pay a reasonable amount of rent on the property!

d) **Barter**

Trade services with your mechanic, barber, lawyer. Of course, you still have the legal obligation to report such benefits as taxable income.

e) **Defer income, accelerate deductions**

When possible, defer increases of income or commission receipts until *after* any determination of support and use Section 179 of the IRS Code to the maximum extent possible to lower your income immediately (deductions for business equipment purchases). See your accountant about paying with a charge card to get the full deduction immediately plus increasing your monthly debt (lowers your income).

f) **Tell your boss you would prefer fringe benefit increases over raises in pay!**

g) **Use one charge card** to pay for all medical expenses not covered by insurance and essentials bought for the children and pay the bill off *monthly* until child support litigation is over. This will normally be allowed to reduce your monthly income when computing child support percentage-based awards.

REDUCING CHILD SUPPORT WITH SSI

If your children are disabled and eligible for SSI (even just with learning or attention problems), your child support may be reduced by the amount of SSI payments. These payments are often very substantial and can in many cases wipe out the child support obligation completely.

MODIFICATION OF CHILD SUPPORT

If your income drops, petition to modify (lower) your child support ***immediately*.** **(See appendix for Petition to Modify).**

You will be held liable for the unmodified level when your ex goes after you for back child support later, after your income increases, if you don't have a *court order* lowering your support.

A verbal or written agreement between you and your ex is worthless. Only a judge can agree to lower your support, because only he protects the child's right to child support. Since child support is the child's, not your ex's, **she cannot agree to lower your support.** She **can agree** to a stipulated order (see appendix form B) for a judge to sign, lowering your support.

CHILD SUPPORT GUIDELINES

States vary widely as to child support formulas. The following statutes from Illinois, Indiana, California and New York are typical.

ILLINOIS FIXED PERCENTAGE

Number of Children	Percent of Supporting Party's Net Income(AFTER TAXES)
1	20%
2	28%
3	32%
4	40%
5	45%
6 or more	50%

CONFUSING CALIFORNIA FORMULA

(there are websites that will calculate this)

The statewide uniform formula for determining child support orders is as follows: CS = K (HN - (H%) (TN)).

(b)(1) The components of the formula are as follows:

a. CS = child support amount.

b. K = amount of both parents' income to be allocated for child support as set forth in paragraph (3).

c. HN = high earner's net monthly disposable income.

d. H% = approximate percentage of time that the high earner has or will have primary physical responsibility for the children compared to the other parent. In cases in which parents have different time-sharing arrangements for different children, H% equals the average of the approximate percentages of time the high earner parent spends with each child.

e. TN = total net monthly disposable income of both parties.

(2) To compute net disposable income, see Section 4059.

(3) K (amount of both parents' income allocated for child support) equals one plus H% (if H% is less than or equal to 50 percent) or two minus H% (if H% is greater than 50 percent) times the following fraction:

Total Net Disposable Income Per Month	K
$0-800	0.20 + TN/16,000
$801-6,666	0.25
$6,667-10,000	0.10 + 1,000/TN
Over $10,000	0.12 + 800/TN

As an example, if H% equals 20 percent and the total monthly net disposable income of the parents is $1,000, K = (1 + 0.20) X 0.25, or 0.30. If H% equals 80 percent and the total monthly net disposable Income of the parents is $1,000, K = (2 - 0.80) X 0.25, or 0.30.

(4) For more than one child, multiply CS by:

2 children	1.6
3 children	2
4 children	2.3
5 children	2.5
6 children	2.625
7 children	2.75
8 children	2.813
9 children	2.844
10 children	2.86

(5) If the amount calculated under the formula results in a positive number, the higher earner shall pay that amount to the lower earner. If the amount calculated under the formula results in a negative number, the lower earner shall pay the absolute value of that amount to the higher earner.

(6) In any default proceeding where proof is by affidavit pursuant to Section 2336, or in any proceeding for child support in which a party fails to appear after being duly noticed, H% shall be set at zero in the formula if the non custodial parent is the higher earner or at 100 if the custodial parent is the higher earner, where there is no evidence presented demonstrating the percentage of time that the non-custodial parent has primary physical responsibility for the children.

(7) In all cases in which the net disposable income per month of the obligor is less than one thousand dollars ($1,000), the court shall rule on whether a low-income adjustment shall be made. The ruling shall be based on the facts presented to the court, the principles provided in Section 4053, and the impact of the contemplated adjustment on the respective net incomes of the obligor and the obligee. Where the court has ruled that a low-income adjustment shall be made, the child support amount otherwise determined under this section shall be reduced by an amount that is no greater than the amount calculated by multiplying the child support amount otherwise determined under this section by a fraction, the numerator of which is 1,000 minus the obligor's net disposable income per month, and the denominator of which is 1,000. If a low-income adjustment is allowed, the court shall state the reasons supporting the adjustment in writing or on the record and shall document the amount of the adjustment and the underlying facts and circumstances.

(8) Unless the court orders otherwise, the order for child support shall allocate the support amount so that the amount of support for the youngest child is the amount of support for one child, and the amount for the next youngest child is the difference between that amount and the amount for two children, with similar allocations for additional children. However, this paragraph does not apply to cases where there are different time-sharing arrangements for different children or where the court determines that the allocation would be inappropriate in the particular case.

(c) In the event a court uses a computer to calculate the child support order, the computer program shall not automatically default affirmatively or negatively on whether a low-income adjustment is to be applied. If the low-income adjustment is applied, the computer program shall not provide the amount of the low-income adjustment. Instead, the computer program shall ask the user whether or not to apply the low-income adjustment, and if answered affirmatively, the computer program shall provide the range of the adjustment permitted by paragraph (7) of subdivision **(b)**.

INDIANA'S INCOMPREHENSIBLE SYSTEM

(a) In an action pursuant to section 3(a), 3(b), or 3(c) of this chapter, the court may order either parent or both parents to pay any amount reasonable for support of a child, without regard to marital misconduct, after considering all relevant factors including:

(1) the financial resources of the custodial parent;
(2) the standard of living the child would have enjoyed had the marriage not been dissolved or had the separation not been ordered;
(3) the physical or mental condition of the child and the child's educational needs; and
(4) the financial resources and needs of the non custodial parent.

(b)The child support order may also include, where appropriate:

(1) sums for the child's education in elementary and secondary schools and at institutions of higher learning, taking into account the child's aptitude and ability and the ability of the parent or parents to meet these expenses;
(2) special medical, hospital, or dental expenses necessary to serve the best interests of the child; and
(3) fees mandated under Title IV-D of the federal Social Security Act.

(c) As part of the child support order the court may set apart such portion of the property of either parent, or both parents, as may seem necessary and proper for the support of the child.

(d) The duty to support a child under this chapter ceases when the child reaches twenty-one (21) years of age unless:

(1) the child is emancipated prior to reaching twenty-one (21) years of age in which case the child support, except for the educational needs outlined in subsection (b)(1), terminates at the time of emancipation; however, an order for educational needs may continue in effect until further order of the court;
(2) the child is incapacitated in which case the child support continues during the incapacity or until further order of the court; or
(3) the child:

(A) is at least eighteen (18) years of age;
(B) has not attended a secondary or post secondary school for the prior four (4) months and is not enrolled in such a school; and
(C) is or is capable of supporting himself through employment; in which case the child support terminates upon the court's finding that the conditions prescribed in this subdivision exist; however, if the court finds that the conditions set forth in clauses (A) through (C) are met but that the child is only partially supporting himself or capable of only partially supporting himself, the court may order that support be modified instead of terminated.

(e) For purposes of determining if a child is emancipated under subsection (d)(1), if the court finds that the child:

(1) has joined the armed services;
(2) has married; or
(3) is not under the care or control of:
(A) either parent; or
(B) an individual or agency approved by the court; the court shall find the child emancipated and terminate the child support

.

(f) The court may, upon a request by the person or agency entitled to receive child support payments, order interest charges of not more than one and one-half percent (1 ½%) per month to be paid on any delinquent child support payment. An application may be made by the person or agency whenever support payments are not made in accordance with the support order. Accrued interest charges may be collected in the same manner as support payments under section 13 of this chapter.

(g) The obligation of a person to pay child support arrearage does not terminate when the person's duty to support a child ceases under subsection (d). The statutes applicable to the collection of child support obligations are applicable to the collection of child support arrearage described by this subsection.

NEW YORK'S NOXIOUS SYSTEM

The amount of the basic child support obligation shall be determined in accordance with the provision of this paragraph:

(1) The court shall determine the combined parental income.

(2) The court shall multiply the combined parental income up to eighty thousand dollars by the appropriate child support percentage and such amount shall be prorated in the same proportion as each parent's income is to the combined parental income.

(3) Where the combined parental income exceeds the dollar amount set forth in subparagraph two of this paragraph, the court shall determine the amount of child support for the amount of the combined parental income in excess of such dollar amount through consideration of the factors set forth in paragraph (f) of this subdivision and/or the child support percentage.

(4) Where the custodial parent is working, or receiving elementary or secondary education, or higher education or vocational training which the court determines will lead to employment, and incurs child care expenses as a result thereof, the court shall determine reasonable child care expenses and such child care expenses, where incurred, shall be prorated in the same proportion as each parent's income is to the combined parental income. Each parent's pro rata share of the child care expenses shall be separately stated and added to the sum of subparagraphs two and three of this paragraph.

(5) The court shall prorate each parent's share of future reasonable health care expenses of the child not covered by insurance in the same proportion as each parent's income is to the combined parental income. The non-custodial parent's pro rata share of such health care expenses shall be paid in a manner determined by the court, including direct payment to the health care provider.

(6) Where the court determines that the custodial parent is seeking work and incurs child care expenses as a result thereof, the court may determine reasonable child care expenses and may apportion the same between the custodial and non-custodial parent. The non-custodial parent's share of such expenses shall be separately stated and paid in a manner determined by the court.

(7) Where the court determines, having regard for the circumstances of the case and of the respective parties and in the best interests of the child, and as justice requires, that the present or future provision of post-secondary, private, special, or enriched education for the child is appropriate, the court may award educational expenses. The non-custodial parent shall pay educational expenses, as awarded, in a manner determined by the court, including direct payment to the educational provider.

(d) Notwithstanding the provisions of paragraph (c) of this subdivision, where the annual amount of the basic child support obligation would reduce the non-custodial parent's income below the poverty income guidelines amount for a single person as reported by the federal department of health and human services, the basic child support obligation shall be twenty-five dollars per month or the difference between the non-custodial parent's income and the self-support reserve, whichever is greater. Notwithstanding the provisions of paragraph (c) of this subdivision, where the annual amount of the basic child support obligation would reduce the non-custodial parent's income below the self-support reserve but not below the poverty income guidelines amount for a single person as reported by the federal department of health and human services, the basic child support obligation shall be fifty dollars per month or the difference between the non-custodial parent's income and the self-support reserve, whichever is greater.

(e) Where a parent is or may be entitled to receive non-recurring payments from extraordinary sources not otherwise considered as income pursuant to this section, including but not limited to:

(1) Life insurance policies;
(2) Discharges of indebtedness;
(3) Recovery of bad debts and delinquency amounts;
(4) Gifts and inheritances; and
(5) Lottery winnings, the court, in accordance with paragraphs (c), (d) and (f) of this subdivision may allocate a proportion of the same to child support, and such amount shall be paid in a manner determined by the court.

(f) The court shall calculate the basic child support obligation, and the non-custodial parent's pro rata share of the basic child support obligation. Unless the court finds that the non-custodial parents's pro-rata share of the basic child support obligation is unjust or inappropriate, which finding shall be based upon consideration of the following factors:

(1) The financial resources of the custodial and non-custodial parent, and those of the child;

(2) The physical and emotional health of the child and his/her special needs and aptitudes;

(3) The standard of living the child would have enjoyed had the marriage or household not been dissolved;

(4) The tax consequences to the parties;

(5) The non-monetary contributions that the parents will make toward the care and well-being of the child;

(6) The educational needs of either parent;

(7) A determination that the gross income of one parent is substantially less than the other parent's gross income;

(8) The needs of the children of the non-custodial parent for whom the non-custodial parent is providing support who are not subject to the instant action and whose support has not been deducted from income pursuant to subclause (D) of clause (vii) of subparagraph five of paragraph (b) of this subdivision, and the financial resources of any person obligated to support such children, provided, however, that this factor may apply only if the resources available to support such children are less than the resources available to support the children who are subject to the instant action;

(9) Provided that the child is not on public assistance (I) extraordinary expenses incurred by the non-custodial parent in exercising visitation, or (ii) expenses incurred by the non-custodial parent in extended visitation provided that the custodial

parent's expenses are substantially reduced as a result thereof; and

(10) Any other factors the court determines are relevant in each case, the court shall order the non-custodial parent to pay his or her pro rata share of the basic child support obligation, and may order the non-custodial parent to pay an amount pursuant to paragraph (e) of this subdivision.

(g) Where the court finds that the non-custodial parent's pro rata share of the basic child support obligation is unjust or inappropriate, the court shall order the non-custodial parent to pay such amount of child support as the court finds just and appropriate, and the court shall set forth, in a written order, the factors it considered; the amount of each party's pro rata share of the basic child support obligation; and the reasons that the court did not order the basic child support obligation. Such written order may not be waived by either party or counsel; provided however, and notwithstanding any other provision of law, including but not limited to section four hundred fifteen of this act, the court shall not find that the non-custodial parent's pro rata share of such obligation is unjust or inappropriate on the basis that such share exceeds the portion of a public assistance grant which is attributable to a child or children. In no instance shall the court order child support below twenty-five dollars per month. Where the non-custodial parent's income is less than or equal to the poverty income guidelines amount for a single person as reported by the federal department of health and human services, unpaid child support arrears in excess of five hundred dollars shall not accrue.

(h) A validly executed agreement or stipulation voluntarily entered into between the parties after the effective date of this subdivision presented to the court for incorporation in an order or judgment shall include a provision stating that the parties have been advised of the provisions of this subdivision and that the basic child support obligation provided for therein would presumptively result in the correct amount of child support to be awarded. In the event that such agreement or stipulation deviates from the basic child support obligation, the agreement or stipulation must specify the amount that such basic child support obligation would have been and the reason or reasons that such agreement or stipulation does not provide for payment of that amount. Such provision may not be waived by either party or counsel. Nothing contained in this subdivision shall be construed to alter the rights of the parties to voluntarily enter into validly executed agreements or stipulations which deviate from the basic child support obligation provided such agreements or stipulations comply with the provisions of this paragraph. The court shall, however, retain discretion with respect to child support pursuant to this section. Any court order or judgment incorporating a validly executed agreement or stipulation which deviates from the basic child support obligation shall set forth the court's reasons for such deviation.

(i) Where either or both parties are unrepresented, the court shall not enter an order or judgment other than a temporary order pursuant to section two hundred thirty-seven of this article, that includes a provision for child support unless the unrepresented party or parties have received a copy of the child support standards chart promulgated by the commissioner of social services pursuant to subdivision two of section one hundred eleven-I of the social services law. Where either party is in receipt of child support enforcement services through the local social services district, the local social services district child support enforcement unit shall advise such party of the amount derived from application of the child support percentage and that such amount serves as a starting point for the determination of the child support award, and shall provide such party with a copy of the child support standards chart. In no instance shall the court approve any voluntary support agreement or compromise that includes an amount for child support less than twenty-five dollars per month.

(j) In addition to financial disclosure required in section four hundred twenty-four-a of this article, the court may require that the income and/or expenses of either party beverified with documentation including, but not limited to, past and present income tax returns, employer statements, pay stubs, corporate, business, or partnership books and records, corporate and business tax returns, and receipts for expenses or such other means of verification as the court determines appropriate. Nothing herein shall affect any party's right to pursue discovery pursuant to this chapter, the civil practice law and rules, or the family court act.

(k) When a party has defaulted and/or the court is otherwise presented with insufficient evidence to determine gross income, the court shall order child support based upon the needs or standard of living of the child, whichever is greater. Such order may be retroactively modified upward, without a showing of change in circumstances.

(l) In any action or proceeding for modification of an order of child support existing prior to the effective date of this paragraph, brought pursuant to article four of this chapter, the child support standards set forth in paragraphs (a) through (k) of this subdivision shall not constitute grounds for modification of such support order; provided, however, that where the circumstances warrant modification of such order, or where an adjustment of a child support order is sought by the support collection unit or either of the parties pursuant to subdivision twelve of section one hundred eleven-h of the social services law, or subdivision three of section four hundred thirteen of the family court act or subdivision four of section two hundred forty of the domestic relations law such standards shall apply. In applying such standards, when the order to be modified incorporates by reference or merges with a validly executed separation agreement or stipulation of settlement, the court may consider, in addition to the factors set forth in paragraph (f) of this subdivision, the provisions of such agreement or stipulation concerning property distribution, distributive award and/or maintenance in determining whether the amount calculated by using the standards would be unjust or inappropriate.

SAFEGUARDING YOUR ASSETS

If possible, don't own anything. Your new spouse or parents or trusted advisor could own assets so that your ex will be discouraged from going after them.

Explore possibilities of setting up corporations or trusts to hold property. The trusts could be arranged to benefit your children. You must seek competent legal advice in this area. It is **NOT** a do-it-yourself area of law!

SAFEGUARDING YOUR SPOUSE'S ASSETS

Execute a pre-nuptial agreement before remarrying, keeping all assets and income separate! Your spouse's assets should be held completely separate from yours, without a showing of change in circumstances, including bank accounts. You should not be able to sign her checks .One joint account could be maintained to pay joint expenses, i.e. food, housing, etc., with each of you contributing a set percentage of the expenses, usually 50/50. Keep this account as *low* as possible. Do not co-mingle savings accounts, mutual funds, etc. Once your money is commingled, it loses its identity and can be considered *all* yours for attachment purposes. Buy luxuries with the new spouses income and keep them in her name. Pay bills from your income.

PROVING CHILD SUPPORT PAYMENTS

Ensure that all of your child support payments be paid through the circuit clerk of the court. The clerk maintains computerized records which will prevent your ex from "forgetting" you paid support.

Invest in a "one-write" checking system that automatically creates a carbon copy entry onto the check register. The SAFEGUARD system is one of several available systems that works well. Keep track of all money spent on your children with ledger entries. ***ALWAYS*** pay by check! The one-write system will also provide you a simple way to prove how you spend your money, an invaluable aid when litigating child support awards and preparing budgets for the court. You should have a column heading to correspond to each expense claimed on your financial statement. (There is a sample statement in the appendix.)

TRICK OF THE TRADE

Save every check you write for child support, or for items you buy for the children, forever and keep a child support log on a monthly basis. Such a log is available from the Fathers' Rights Foundation at http://www.fathers-rights.com .

PREVENTING SEIZURE OF YOUR TAX REFUND

If you are found to be behind in child support, you can count on your tax refund being taken each year. The solution to this is to claim the maximum number of exemptions allowable, so that you are not overpaying your taxes (the only reason for a refund). See your employer to adjust your deductions. If you are self-employed, calculate your quarterly payments more carefully so as to eliminate overpayment without incurring underpayment penalties. Make sure your spouse also takes the maximum exemptions if you are filing a joint return!

FIGHTING OUT-OF-STATE SUPPORT ORDERS

If you are served with a notice from your local State's Attorney or agency attempting to collect an award of child support from out of state, use the arguments in the brief in the Appendix. This process often causes delays of up to years.

Also, don't forget, most agencies or States' Attorneys cannot represent one spouse on the issues of visitation or custody. The issue of child support cannot be decided if the issue of custody is again raised. Custody must be determined first! Consider filing for custody if your ex is neglecting your children financially.

If your ex is going to cause you to incur attorney fees, you might as well resolve all of your visitation and custody problems at the same court hearings and force her to pay for her attorney! Always file a counter-petition in response to any petition she files. The best defense is a good offense.

Most out-of-state orders can be negotiated with your local State's Attorney to a very low payment on any arrearage. These local assistant State's Attorneys or prosecutors are covered up with child support collection cases and will readily agree to low payments just to clear a case off the books. I have seen $25,000 in arrearage set for repayment at $10 per month, after the father insisted that the *full discovery* process described in the following pages be completed before the hearing! Insist on your full legal rights to contest custody and support. The Federal Government encourages states to go after fathers by publishing collection hints. Some of their recommended tactics are in the appendix. Read them and be forewarned. It is of note that nowhere does the government give advice on enforcing visitation despite statistics proving that when visitation is given, support is usually paid.

DISCOVERY

If your ex is attempting to increase your child support, you have a right to determine her financial condition through a process called discovery. To litigate without discovery is almost malpractice per se. Anyone claiming child support or trying to collect support *must* complete the time-consuming and expensive discovery process described below! Of course, it would be unethical to insist on discovery simply to harass your opponent! Some discovery tools are:

a) Depositions

1) In a deposition, the party is put under oath and asked questions to determine what they are going to say in court. Depositions are expensive and time-consuming. You must pay attorneys and a court reporter. **Often, the costs of depositions deter a party from pursuing claims.**

TRICK OF THE TRADE

1) If you are deposed, here are some useful hints:

i) Pay attention to your physical appearance. It is important that you make a good impression on the opposing counsel and the opposing party. You should dress as if you were actually going to court. You should be clean and wear clean, neat clothing.

ii) Treat all persons in the deposition room with respect. Do not be afraid of the lawyers.

iii) Speak slowly and clearly.

iv) Tell the truth. Do not try to figure out before you answer whether a truthful answer will help or hinder your case. Many questions you will be asked will not be admissible at trial, but the opposition is entitled to an answer in order to help prepare its case. Many cases are lost because a witness tries to hide something. Many of the questions cannot be used in the trial unless you have not told the truth and your false answers can be shown at the trial.

v) Never state anything as a fact that you do not know. There is, however, a distinction between a guess and an honest estimate.

*vi) **Do not volunteer** any facts not requested.*

vii) Do not try to memorize your testimony.

viii) Do not answer a question unless you have heard it and clearly understand it. Ask for the question to be repeated, or if necessary for a minute to think.

*ix) Answer all questions directly, giving concise answers to the questions and **STOP TALKING**.*

*x) If your attorney begins to speak, **stop** whatever answer you may be giving and allow him or her to make the statement.*

xi) Do not let the opposing attorney get you angry or excited.

TRICK OF THE TRADE

Go to the bathroom if you get in trouble.

xii) Never joke in a deposition.

xiii) After the deposition is over, do not chat with the opponent or her attorney. **LEAVE**!

TRICK OF THE TRADE

When deposing your ex, make sure her attorney isn't sitting so close she can kick your ex to stop her from talking. This is very unethical.

b) Interrogatories

Interrogatories are written questions submitted to a party that must be answered and returned. They are useful to keep the other party from changing their story or surprising you in court. Sample interrogatories are in the appendix to this book.

c) Requests to Admit

These are sent to your ex to narrow the issues so you don't have to prove everything in court, saving *a lot* of time and legal fees!

d) Request to Produce Documents

These force the other side to produce records you need in court or records they intend to use against you.

UNWED FATHERS

Unwed fathers are often held liable for birth and maternity expenses and usually held liable for payment of child support as if you were married.

Some states, however, have attempted to limit unwed fathers' rights while still requiring them to pay child support. It is imperative that as soon as a child is born, the father file a petition to determine paternity to establish future father's rights, **even if you are currently living with the mother**! Remember, there is no presumption that the mother will get custody if you choose to seek custody! The unwed father, once determined to be the father, has almost the same rights as if the couple were married including the right to custody! Unwed fathers are winning custody more and more often!

WITHHOLDING ORDERS,

Layoffs, and Modification of Support

If child support is awarded, most states now require that an order of withholding be sent to your employer. Your employer will send the child support automatically to the court clerk. **If you are laid off and child support is temporarily interrupted, you must either pay the payments yourself or *immediately* file a Petition to Modify (lower) Child Support.** You will be granted your petition, often with the family portion of any unemployment benefits being designated as full child support. Of course, you must pay that amount each month *and keep detailed records and receipts.* The Fathers' Rights Foundation's Visitation and Support Log is a useful tool for keeping these records handy for use in the courtroom. If you don't petition the court to lower your support payments, you can count on having to pay all back payments up to date when you get back to work! An agreement between you and your ex or any state agency is **meaningless**. You **must** have a written and signed court order lowering your support. **ONLY** a judge can lower child support!

SUMMARY

The foregoing ideas, coupled with the documents in the appendix will enable you to fight unreasonable demands by litigating the support question to the same extent as any other issues litigated in court.

You are entitled to fully use the legal system and all of its procedures and protections.

Your ex is using the system against you. You are entitled to use the system and due process safeguards to oppose her in any ethical way possible.

By fighting awards in unreasonable child support, often given without any accounting protection to make sure the money is spent on the children, a father in this way can ensure that at least some of his money is spent directly on his children's best interests.

To prevail, however, you probably will need competent, aggressive, legal counsel. If your ex has counsel and you don't, you will almost certainly fail. However, just making litigation an unpleasant and expensive battle may prevent the ex from coming back the *next* time for more money!

WHAT THE FEDS ARE DOING TO COLLECT SUPPORT:

At no time in history have the feminists wielded such power in Washington as now. Women are attempting to criminalize divorce, and men are the criminals! Debtors' prisons are a reality for men who can't prove they pay their support.

It may be useful to know to what extent the Federal Government is involved in helping states enforce child support and their recommended tactics . Below are copies of actual government documents:

ACF/OCSE Fact Sheet

Office of Child Support Enforcement
Program Description

The goal of the Child Support Enforcement (CSE) Program, which was established in 1975 under Title IV-D of the Social Security Act, is to ensure that children are financially supported by both their parents. Recent laws,

including the Family Support Act of 1988, provide for strong child support enforcement measures to assure that parental responsibility is met.

The CSE program is usually run by state and local human services departments, often with the help of prosecuting attorneys, other law enforcement agencies, and officials of family or domestic relations courts.

Child Support Enforcement services are available automatically for families receiving assistance under Aid to Families with Dependent Children (AFDC) programs. A family receives up to the first $50 of any current child support each month without a decrease in the AFDC payment. Any remainder reimburses the state and federal governments for AFDC payments made to the family. AFDC recipients must assign to the state any rights to support that they or eligible children may have.

Child support services are also available to families not receiving AFDC who apply for such services. Child support payments that are collected on behalf of non-AFDC families are sent to the family. For these families, states must charge an application fee of up to $25, but may pay such fee from state funds. Some states may also charge for the cost of services rendered.

The most recent census data show that, in the Spring of 1992, 11.5 million families with children had a parent living elsewhere. Custodial parent families, 86 percent of which were headed by women and 14 percent headed by men, comprised one third of all families with their own, never married children under 21. Of the 11.5 million, only 6.2 million (54 percent) of the custodial parents had awards or agreements for child support. Of the total $17.7 billion owed for child support in 1991, $5.8 billion was not paid. Among those due support, about half received the full amount, about a quarter received partial payment and about a quarter received nothing.

During FY 1994, about $10 billion in child support payments was collected through the Program. Paternity was established for more than 590,000 children that year, clearing the way for the establishment of child support orders and other vital links between the children and their non-custodial parents.

There are four major services provided by the Child Support Enforcement Program:

* **Locating Absent Parents**
* **Establishing Paternity**
* **Establishing Child Support Obligations**
* **Enforcing Child Support Orders**

Locating Absent Parents -- Child support enforcement officials use local information and resources of State and Federal Parent Locator services to locate parents for child support enforcement, or to find a parent in parental kidnaping/custody disputes.

These resources include:

STATE	FEDERAL
Motor Vehicles/Drivers Licenses	Internal Revenue Service
Employment/Unemployment Records	Department of Defense
State Income Tax	Social Security
Public Assistance Records	Veterans Administration
Selective Service System	
Federal Civilian Personnel Records	

About four million cases are processed annually by the Federal Parent Locator Service. The FPLS provides an address in approximately 80 percent of the cases submitted.

<u>Establishing Paternity</u> -- Establishing paternity (legally identifying a child's father) is a necessary first step for obtaining an order for child support when children are born out of wedlock. Establishing paternity also provides access to:

- **Social security, pension and retirement benefits;**
- **Health insurance and information; and**
- **Interaction with members of both parents' families.**

Many fathers voluntarily acknowledge paternity. Otherwise, father, mother and child can be required to submit to genetic tests. The results are highly accurate. States must have procedures which allow paternity to be established at least up to the child's eighteenth birthday.

<u>Establishing Support Obligations</u> -- States must have guidelines to establish how much a parent should pay for child support. Support agency staff can take child support cases to court, or to an administrative hearing process to establish the order. Health insurance coverage can also be ordered.

<u>Enforcing Child Support Orders</u> -- A parent can be required to pay child support by income withholding -- money held out of the paycheck by the employer and sent to the child support office or court. Overdue child support can be collected from federal and state income tax refunds. Liens can be put on property, and the property itself may even be sold with the proceeds used to pay child support arrearage. Unpaid child support can be reported to credit bureaus so that a parent who owes child support may have trouble making purchases on credit.

ACF/OCSE Fact Sheet

Child Support Enforcement Steps

The Child Support Enforcement (CSE) Program is a federal/state/local effort to locate parents, their employers, and/or their assets; establish paternity if necessary; and establish and enforce child support orders. State and local CSE offices provide day to day operation of the program. The federal role is to provide funding, issue policies, ensure that federal requirements are met, and interact with other federal agencies that help support the CSE program.

How and where do I apply?

In most states, CSE offices are listed under the human services agency in the local government section of the telephone directory. If there is not a separate listing, the human services agency information operator should be able to give you the number. State CSE agencies are listed at the end of this brochure; they also can provide telephone numbers for local offices.

Call your Child Support Enforcement office to learn how to apply for enforcement services and what documents (birth certificates, financial statements, etc.) you should provide.

What are the steps to collecting support?

The first step, if a child was born out of wedlock, is to establish paternity - or make a legal determination of who fathered the child. Many men will voluntarily acknowledge paternity. Either parent can request a blood test in contested paternity cases. Your caseworker will help you to establish paternity for your child.

Establishing the obligation is the next step. The fair amount of child support that the non-custodial parent should pay is determined according to state guidelines. Your CSE office will be able to tell you how support award amounts are set in your state. Your CSE office can also request medical support for your child.

The last step is enforcement of the child support order. The CSE office can help with collecting the money due no matter where the non-custodial parent lives.

At any of these steps, the CSE office may need to know where the non-custodial parent is living or where he/she is working. When a parent has disappeared, it is usually possible for the CSE office to find him/her with the help of state agencies, such as the Department of Motor Vehicles, or the Federal Parent Locator Service. Your caseworker can tell you what information is needed to find an absent parent or his/her employer.

The most successful way to collect child support is by direct withholding from the obligated parent's paycheck. Most child support orders require the employer to withhold the money that is ordered for child support and send it to the CSE office. Your Child Support Enforcement office can tell you about this procedure.

Federal and State Income Tax refunds may be withheld to collect unpaid child support. States also have laws which allow them to use: liens on real and personal property; orders to withhold and deliver property; or seizure and sale of property with the proceeds applied to the support debt. Many states routinely report child support debts to credit bureaus and smart parents are bringing their payments current so that their credit won't be affected.

For more information, write for the Handbook on Child Support Enforcement.

STATE CHILD SUPPORT ENFORCEMENT AGENCIES

Alabama	(205) 242-9300
Alaska	(907) 276-3441
Arizona	(602) 252-0236
Arkansas	(501) 682-8398
California	(916) 654-1556
Colorado	(303) 866-5994
Connecticut	(203) 566-3053
Delaware	(302) 577-4863
DC	(202) 724-8800
Florida	(904) 488-9900
Georgia	(404) 657-3851
Guam	(671) 475-3360
Hawaii	(808) 587-3700
Idaho	(208) 334-5710
Illinois	(217) 782-8768
Indiana	(317) 2324894
Iowa	(515) 281-5580
Kansas	(913) 296-3237
Kentucky	(502) 564-2285
Louisiana	(504) 342-4780
Maine	(207) 287-2886
Maryland	(410) 333-3979
Massachusetts	(617) 727-4200
Michigan	(517) 373-7570
Minnesota	(612) 296-2542
Mississippi	(601) 359-4500
Missouri	(314) 751-4301
Montana	(406) 444-4614
Nebraska	(402) 471-9125
Nevada	(702) 687-4744
New Hampshire	(603)2 714426
New Jersey	(609) 588-2361
New Mexico	(505) 827-7200
New York	(518) 474-9081
North Carolina	(919) 571-4120
North Dakota	(701) 224-3582
Ohio	(614) 752-6561
Oklahoma	(405) 424-5871
Oregon	(503) 986-2417
Pennsylvania	(717) 787-3672
Puerto Rico	(809) 722-4731
Rhode Island	(401) 277-2409
South Carolina	(803) 737-5870
South Dakota	(605) 773-3641
Tennessee	(615) 741-1820
Texas	(512) 463-2181
Utah	(801) 538-4400
Vermont	(802) 241-2319
Virgin Islands	(809) 774-5666
Virginia	(804) 692-2458
Washington	(206) 586-3162
West Virginia	(304) 558-3780
Wisconsin	(608) 266-9909
Wyoming	(307) 777-6948

UIFSA

Your state had probably adopted or will adopt the new UIFSA collection act. This insidious act is probably unconstitutional since it gives foreign states jurisdiction over citizens of different states in a manner previously ruled unconstitutional by the U.S. Supreme Court.

§ 750 ILCS 22/502. Employer's compliance with income-withholding order of another state :

Sec. 502. Employer's compliance with income-withholding order of another state.

(a)Upon receipt of an income-withholding order, the obligor's employer shall immediately provide a copy of the order to the obligor.

(b)The employer **shall treat an income-withholding order issued in another state which appears regular on its face as if it had been issued by a tribunal of this State.**

(c) Except as otherwise provided in subsection

(d) and Section 503 [750 ILCS 22/503] the employer shall withhold and distribute the funds as directed in the withholding order by complying with terms of the order which specify:

(1) the duration and amount of periodic payments of current child-support, stated as a sum certain;

(2) the person or agency designated to receive payments and the address to which the payments are to be forwarded;

(3) medical support, whether in the form of periodic cash payment, stated as a sum certain, or ordering the obligor to provide health insurance coverage for the child under a policy available through the obligor's employment;

(4) the amount of periodic payments of fees and costs for a support enforcement agency, the issuing tribunal, and the obligee's attorney, stated as sums certain; and

(5) the amount of periodic payments of arearages and interest on arearages, stated as sums certain.

(d) An employer shall comply with the law of the state of the obligor's principal place of employment for withholding from income with respect to:

(1) the employer's fee for processing an income-withholding order;

(2) the maximum amount permitted to be withheld from the obligor's income; and

(3) the times within which the employer must implement the withholding order and forward the child support payment.

History (Source: P.A. 88-550, § 502; 90-240, § 5.)

TRICK OF THE TRADE

The following forms have been successfully used to defeat collection efforts under the UIFSA Act and the older URISA Act.

IN THE CIRCUIT COURT OF THE 1ST
JUDICIAL CIRCUIT, GENERIC COUNTY, ILLINOIS

In Re: The Marriage of:	)	
JOHN DOE	)	
Petitioner	)	
and	)	CASE NO: 88-F-99
	)	
CYNTHIA JEAN DOE,	)	
Respondent.	)	

PETITION FOR INJUNCTIVE RELIEF AND TO ENFORCE SETTLEMENT

NOW COMES the Respondent, John Anthony DOE, by and through his attorney, Ronald L. Isaacs, and for his Petition For Injunctive Relief And To Enforce Settlement states as follows:

1. On or about March 29, 1988, a Consent Order and an Order For Withholding were filed in the above-entitled matter, which established the Respondent's arrearage at $5,378.22 and ordered the Respondent to pay child support in the amount of $39.00 per week and to retire said arrearage at the rate of $8.00 per week. See Exhibit A, attached.

2. On or about May 31, 1995 the state of Minnesota issued an unregistered "order"/notice to the Respondent for direct enforcement under Minnesota Statute 518.611, Subdivision 2,(UIFSA) which threatened and instructed the Respondent's employer to withhold $128.00 per month on arrears alleged to be in the amount of $38, 924.84. Said notice does not even appear to be signed by a Judge (see Exhibit B, attached), yet Plaintiff's employer is following the notice from Minnesota vice the Illinois Orders.

3. Respondent has been denied all due process by the state of Minnesota and received no notices of any hearings to determine any arrearage or child support owed in Minnesota.

4. As required by 750 ILCS 22/501, on November 25, 1996 Respondent filed a challenge with Minnesota as to the validity of its "order" (see Exhibit C, attached).

5. Cynthia Jean DOE is bound by the *Illinois* Consent Order. Cynthia Jean DOE submitted herself to the jurisdiction of Illinois to obtain said Consent Order.

6. John Anthony DOE is current in his child support under the Illinois Consent Order.

7. 750 ILCS 22/501 is **unconstitutional on its face** in that it subjects a person from this state to the jurisdiction of a foreign state without any requirement of minimum contacts or safeguard of due process as is required for registered orders which must proceed through Illinois courts and which are not enforceable in Illinois if due process was not granted by the issuing state.

WHEREFORE the Respondent moves the Court to enforce its judgment of March 29, 1988, to enjoin Plaintiff's employer to follow the Illinois Consent Order only, and for such further relief the Court deems equitable and just.

____

John Anthony DOE,

Carbondale, IL 62901

PROOF OF SERVICE

The undersigned certifies that a copy of the foregoing instrument was served upon:

Tina Doe, Child Support Officer
Carlton County Human Services
Center 300 Main
1215 Avenue C
Cloquet, MN 55720

Office of Illinois Attorney General
100 Main
Quincy Illinois

by enclosing the same in an envelope addressed as shown above, with postage fully prepaid, and by depositing said envelope in a U.S. Post Office mailbox in Alton Illinois, on the_______ day of ______________________, 2000_.

STATE OF ILLINOIS
IN THE CIRCUIT COURT OF THE_____JUDICIAL CIRCUIT
__________COUNTY, ILLINOIS

ILLINOIS DEPARTMENT OF PUBLIC AID, ex rel.	)	
______________________, Petitioner,	)	
	)	CASE ____
Respondent.	)	

MOTION TO DISMISS FOR LACK OF JURISDICTION, NOTICE, OR SERVICE OF PROCESS

NOW COMES ________________ by and through his attorney, __________________________, and for his Motion to Dismiss for lack of Jurisdiction respectfully states as follows:

1. ____________________ does not have the requisite minimum contacts with the State of Ohio to cause Jurisdiction to exist over him by that State.

2. ______________________ was never notified of any hearing on this matter in Ohio, never served with process or notice of hearing during which the Ohio order was issued.

WHEREFORE Respondent moves this Court to Dismiss for lack of Jurisdiction and for such other relief the Court deems just.

____

VERIFICATION

Under penalties as provided by law pursuant to Section 1-109 of the Code of Civil Procedure, the undersigned certifies that the statements set forth in this instrument are true and correct, except as to matters therein stated to be on information and belief and as to such matters the undersigned certifies as aforesaid that he verily believes the same to be true.

____

PROOF OF SERVICE

The undersigned certifies that a copy of the foregoing instrument was served upon the attorneys of record of all parties to the above cause by enclosing the same in an envelope addressed to such attorneys at their business address as disclosed by the pleadings of record herein, with postage fully prepaid and by depositing said envelope in the U.S. Post Office mail box in Carbondale, Illinois, on the _____ day of ___________________, 2002.

____
Attorney at Law

STATE OF ILLINOIS
IN THE CIRCUIT COURT OF THE_____JUDICIAL CIRCUIT________COUNTY, ILLINOIS

ILLINOIS DEPARTMENT	)	
OF PUBLIC AID, ex rel.	)	
	)	
Petitioner,	)	
	)	
v.	)	CASE :
	)	
	)	
____________________	)	
Respondent.	)	
	)	

ORDER

This cause coming before the Court on the Motion of the Respondent to Dismiss for lack of Jurisdiction. The Court having considered the Motion and pleadings of counsel, finds the allegations of the Motion are supported by the facts abduced in support thereof and;

IT IS HEREBY ORDERED that this cause be, and same is hereby, **Granted.**

____

JUDGE

DATED:_______________________________

TRICK OF THE TRADE

THE FOLLOWING MEMO RESULTED IN A FOREIGN STATE SIMPLY GIVING UP ON COLLECTING ON A BOGUS ORDER FROM THEIR STATE:

STATE OF ILLINOIS
IN THE CIRCUIT COURT OF THE_____JUDICIAL CIRCUIT
________________ COUNTY, ILLINOIS

ILLINOIS DEPARTMENT	)	
OF PUBLIC AID, ex rel.	)	
________________________,	)	
Petitioner,	)	
	)	
v.	)	CASE _
	)	
________________________	)	
Respondent.	)	

MEMORANDUM OF LAW IN SUPPORT OF MOTION TO DISMISS

NOW COMES __________________, by and through his attorney, __________________, and for his Memorandum of Law in Support of Motion to Dismiss for lack of Jurisdiction respectfully states as follows:

1. This action was brought under the Revised Uniform Reciprocal Enforcement of Support Act seeking to enforce an Ohio Order.

2. Section 20/40 - Enforcement Procedures states:

§ 750 ILCS 20/40. Effect of Registration; Enforcement Procedure.

Sec. 40. Effect of Registration; Enforcement Procedure.
(a) Upon registration the registered foreign support order shall be treated in the same manner as a support order entered by a court of this State. **It has the same effect and is subject to the same procedures, defenses, and proceedings for reopening, vacating, or staying as a support order of this State and may be enforced and satisfied in like manner.**

(b) The obligor has 30 days after the mailing of notice of the registration in which to petition the court to vacate the registration or for other relief. If he does not so petition the registered support order is confirmed.

(c) At the hearing to enforce the registered support order the obligor may present only matters that would be available to him as defenses in an action to enforce a foreign money judgment. If he shows to the court that an appeal from the order is pending or will be taken or that a stay of enforcement has been granted the court shall stay enforcement of the order until the appeal is concluded, the time for appeal has expired, or the order is vacated, upon satisfactory proof that the obligor has furnished security for payment of the support ordered as required by the rendering state. If he shows to the court any ground upon which enforcement of a support order of this State may be stayed the court shall stay enforcement of the order for an appropriate period if the obligor furnishes the same security for payment of the support ordered that is required for a support order of this State.

3. The available defenses of Respondent to this action are under the Foreign Judgments Recognition Act 735 ILCS 5/12-621 Sections (a.), (a.)1 and (a.)2 and (b), (b.)1 and (b.)4.

§ 735 ILCS 5/12-621. Inconclusiveness of judgments.
Sec. 12-621. Inconclusiveness of judgments. (a)A foreign judgment is not conclusive if

(1) the judgment was rendered under a system which does not provide impartial tribunals or procedures compatible with the requirements of due process of law;
(2) the foreign court did not have personal jurisdiction over the defendant; or
(3) the foreign court did not have jurisdiction over the subject matter.

(b) A foreign judgment need not be recognized if

(1) the defendant in the proceedings in the foreign court did not receive notice of the proceedings in sufficient time to enable him or her to defend;
(2) the judgment was obtained by fraud;
(3) the cause of action on which the judgment is based is repugnant to the public policy of this State;
(4) the judgment conflicts with another final and conclusive judgment;
(5) the proceeding in the foreign court was contrary to an agreement between the parties under which the dispute in question was to be settled otherwise than by proceedings in that court; or
(6) in the case of jurisdiction based only on personal service, the foreign court was a seriously inconvenient forum for the trial of the action.

4. Respondents Defenses under (a.), (a.)1 and (a.) 2:

On the face of the order and exhibits attached and rendered by the Ohio Court, no evidence of any notice of any hearing determining the claimed arrearage and resulting in the January 25, 1995 Order is presented. Respondent had no notice of said hearing and thus was not provided procedures compatible with the requirements of due process of law as required by Section 5/12-621 (a). Neither was service obtained gaining personal jurisdiction to require Respondents presence before the Court as required by 5/12-621(b).

5. Respondents Defense under Section 5/12-621(b)(1):

Respondent received no Notice of the Ohio Courts hearing on January 25, 1995 of the Petition for arrearage.

6. Respondents Defense under 5/12-621 (b)(2):

The Order rendered is clearly in error and contradicts that Ohio Courts previous Order of August 30, 1994 that set the payment of Child Support with arrearage at $50.00 per month and states this modification shall be in effect until obligor becomes gainfully employed. The affidavit of Respondent is attached stating he is a student and not gainfully employed.

7. Page 2 of 2 of the Uniform Support Petition contains erasures attempting to conceal figures that reflect the Courts Order of August 30, 1994 and said changes are not initialed or dated. The new figures differ from the original figures entered which match the figures of the August 30, 1994 order.

8. Respondent does not in fact owe any back child support but has in fact overpaid child support by approximately $2000.00 because of an error in withholding from his pay and Plaintiff was well aware that she has received said overpayment.

WHEREFORE Respondent moves the Court deny enforcement of the foreign Order of the Ohio Court.

By:______________________________

____
ATTORNEY AT LAW
____
____

<u>USE THIS TO LOWER SUPPORT AND INCREASE VISITATION</u>

STATE OF ILLINOIS
IN THE CIRCUIT COURT OF THE _____ JUDICIAL CIRCUIT
________________ COUNTY, ILLINOIS

IN RE THE MARRIAGE OF

etc:

PETITION TO MODIFY

NOW COMES the Defendant, ______________________, by and through his attorney, __________________________________, and prays this Court modify a Judgment of Dissolution of Marriage and in support thereof respectfully states as follows:

1. On December 15, 1983, this Court entered a judgment of Dissolution of marriage, which Judgment has not been modified or rescinded.

2. As part of the said Judgment of Dissolution of Marriage, the Court ordered in paragraph 9 in words as figures as follows;

> "Defendant is to pay to Plaintiff as and for the support of the minor children the sum of $300.00 per month per child. Payments are to be made through the Circuit Clerks office in two equal monthly installments of $300.00, due and payable on the first installment due and payable on December 1, 1983."

3. That said Judgment in paragraph 2 ordered:
"That the Plaintiff, __________________, shall have the care, custody, and control and education of the minor children of the parties, namely: ________ and ___________, and is granted leave to remove the children from the State of Illinois to the State of Alabama where she intends to reside. The Defendant is granted visitation as follows:
    a) Four consecutive weeks during the summer;
    b) One week during the children's Christmas break from school;
    c) One week during the children's spring break from school;
    d) At such other times as Defendant is in Alabama, not to exceed two consecutive days at any one time;
    e) At such times as Plaintiff is in Illinois with the Children, but not to exceed three consecutive days at any one time;
    f) Defendant is required to give Plaintiff 30 days advance notice, in writing, of the date he intends to pick up the children for the summer visitation, and at least one week's oral or written notice when he intends to see the children in Alabama.
    g) The Plaintiff is to give the Defendant at least three weeks oral or written notice when the children will have their Christmas and Spring break and at least one week oral and written notice of when the children will be in Southern Illinois."

And;

"7. Plaintiff has a specific duty to turn over the children to Defendant or his representative for his visitation even though the children may object to such visitation."

4. ________________________, one of the two children of the parties, became 18 years of age in May 2000.

5. Defendant should not be required to pay child support to Plaintiff for the support of _____________________ after May, 2000.

6. Based on the information and belief of the Defendant, ___________________________, one of the two children of the parties, is eligible for SSI payments and that the SSI payments should offset any support obligations by either party.

7. That Plaintiff has failed to facilitate the relationship between Defendant and his children by denying visitation and it is in the best interests of the child that the court order custody be changed and awarded to Defendant, with reasonable child support.

WHEREFORE Defendant prays this court:

A. Change Custody from Plaintiff to Defendant, with Plaintiff paying reasonable child support.

B. Award the tax deduction for the children to Defendant,

C. Require the custodial parent to file for and obtain SSI payments.

D. That SSI payments offset any child support obligation of any party.

E. That if custody is not awarded to Defendant that visitation be increased and that makeup visitation be ordered day for day.

F. That the child support provision for ______________ be terminated.

G. For such other relief the court deems just and equitable.

____

Attorney at Law

VERIFICATION

The undersigned, being first duly sworn on oath deposes and states that the contents of the foregoing document are true (except as to matter alleged to be on information and belief and those he believes to be true).

____

____

Subscribed and sworn to before me this __________ day of __________________, 2000.

____

Notary Public

STATE OF _________)
) **SS.**
COUNTY OF _______)

AFFIDAVIT

I, ____________________________________, certify that I have read the foregoing document and that to the best of my knowledge, information, and belief formed after reasonable inquiry it is well grounded in fact and is warranted by existing law or a good faith argument for the extension, modification, or reversal of existing law and that it is not interposed for any improper purpose, such as to harass or to cause unnecessary delay or a needless increase in the cost of litigation. All facts plead therein are herein incorporated.

Subscribed and sworn to before me this __________ day of __________________, 2002

____

Notary Public

THE FOLLOWING DISCOVERY DOCUMENTS HAVE ALLOWED SPACE SO THEY MAY BE DUPLICATED FOR YOUR USE.

IN THE CIRCUIT COURT OF THE ______ JUDICIAL CIRCUIT ____________COUNTY, ILLINOIS

In Re: The Marriage of:	)	
	)	
________________________,	)	
	)	
Petitioner,	)	
and	)	
	)	CASE
	)	
___________________,	)	
	)	
Respondent.	)	

INTERROGATORIES

COMES NOW the Petitioner, _________________, by and through his undersigned attorney, and propounds the attached Interrogatories to the Respondent, to be answered under oath within twenty eight (28) days from the date of service thereof, pursuant to Supreme Court Rule 213.

INSTRUCTIONS

Please insert your answers in the space provided following each question. If additional space is needed, so indicate in the space provided, and prepare your answer on a separate paper and attach.

INTERROGATORIES TO (insert name)

A. Please state your full name, address, date of birth and social security number.

B. Please describe your current employment including the names and address of your present employer and, the dates of your employment and the nature of your job.

C. With regard to your income, please state the following:

a. State your gross annual earned income, from all sources, for each of the last three years. Identify source and amount from each source.

b. State when you are paid and indicate for each pay period your gross salary and wages, itemize the deductions from your gross salary wages and your net salary or wages.

c. Set forth any additional compensation, including but not limited to, overtime, bonuses, profit sharing, insurance, expense account, automobile or automobile allowance, which you have received from your employer or anticipate receiving.

d. State your total annual income in each of the past three years.

e. Itemize all other income or support payments received.

D. With regard to your assets, please state:

a. Describe by legal description and addresses all real property which you own, or in which you have an interest, setting forth the percentage of your interest in each parcel. For each parcel, state date of purchase, purchase price and present market value.

b List the names and addresses of all persons or entities which own an interest with you in the parcels of real property described in the foregoing sub-paragraph and describe such interest.

c List all of the items of tangible personal property, including but not limited to, motor vehicles, furniture, boats, jewelry or art objects which are owned by you or in which you have an interest. State your estimate of value for each item.

d. List the names and addresses of the persons who own an interest with you in the items of tangible personal property described in the foregoing sub-paragraph and describe such interest.

e. List all accounts in which you have deposited money in your name or jointly with another person within the last 12 months.

E. As to the accounts set forth in the foregoing answer, set forth the account numbers, the cash balances and the persons and their addresses who are authorized to withdraw funds in said account.

F. List all intangible personal property, including but not limited to, stocks, bonds and mortgages owned by you or in which you have an interest within the last two years. State percentage of your interest and the present value of each interest.

G. List the names and addresses of persons or entities indebted to you and state the nature and amount of their obligations to you.

H. List all other assets which you own, having an interest in or the use and benefit of, setting forth your interest and value thereof.

I. Describe in detail, including the cash value, all insurance policies of which you are the owner or beneficiary, including but not limited to health, disability and life insurance. As to each policy, list the issuing insurance company and policy number.

4. With regard to your liabilities, please list all liabilities, debts and other obligations, all credit cards issued to you, indicating for each whether it is secured or unsecured, and, if secured, the nature of the security, setting forth the payment schedule as to each and the name and address of each creditor, the balances owed and present monthly payments and the account numbers for each account.

5. With regard to your living expenses, please complete the attached statement of financial affairs.

6. State the amount of money contributed monthly, directly or indirectly, for the support of your spouse or other dependents for the past year next preceding the answers to these Interrogatories.

7. State the condition of your health and the name and address of all health care providers who have examined or treated you within the last 3 years.. State the same information for each child, if any.

8. Please specify on what facts you base your claim for child custody.

9. Please describe in detail events or other facts which lead you to believe that you will be a better custodian of the minor child than your spouse.

10. Please describe with the particularity the events or facts which lead you to believe that your spouse is not equipped or otherwise prepared to be the custodial parent of the minor child.

11. Will you please specify the facts upon which you rely to support your allegations that you would be a fit and proper person to have the care, custody and control of the minor child and can provide a better environment for the minor child to live in.

12. Please describe in detail your daily and/or social habits, including, but not limited to:

a) Alcohol use;
b) Drug use;
c) Participation in sports;
d) Attendance at theater, lecture, museums, etc.;
e) Attendance at social gatherings, such as parties, etc.
f) Attendance at church activities;

13. Describe in specific terms, your relationship with the child which qualifies you for custody of the child. Include in your answer your past record with response to visits with the child, time spent with him, the quality of custodial care provided for him by you in the past and interest shown in the child's daily life.

14. Describe in detail the kind of household you propose to provide to the child as a custodial parent. Include in your answer where the household is to be maintained.

15. State the name and address or otherwise identify and locate all persons who have knowledge of the facts and circumstances concerning custody or who will be called as witnesses, either in you behalf or adverse to you and describe the facts to which each said person has knowledge or will testify.

16. For anyone who has provided child care for the minor child(ren), state the following:

a. Name

b. Address

c. Telephone Number

d. Licensing or credentials

e. Dates of child care

f. Location of Child care

g. Purpose for use of child care

17. If you have alleged grounds for divorce, state the following:

a. Dates of occurrences;

b. Places of occurrences;

c. Persons present.

18. If you have made any contribution to the acquisition, preservation or increase in the value of marital or non marital property, please state:

a. What the contribution was;

b. When the contribution was.

19. If you have any vocational skills or vocational qualifications please describe them.

CERTIFICATION

Under penalties as provided by law pursuant to Section 1-109 of the code of Civil Procedure, the undersigned certifies that the statements set forth in this Petition are true and correct, except as to matters stated to be on information and belief, and as to those matters, the undersigned certifies as stated that he verily believes them to be true.

____

____

IN THE CIRCUIT COURT OF THE ____________JUDICIAL CIRCUIT
_______________ COUNTY, ILLINOIS

In Re: The Marriage of:	)	
	)	
________________________,	)	
	)	
Petitioner,	)	
and	)	
	)	CASE:
	)	
__________________,	)	
	)	
Respondent.	)	

REQUEST TO PRODUCE

COMES NOW Petitioner/Husband, ______________________________, by and through his undersigned attorneys, pursuant to Rules of Civil Procedure, and requests that the Respondent/Wife, produce and permit the Petitioner/Husband to inspect and to copy each of the following documents:

INSTRUCTIONS

1. You are requested to supplement your answers to this Request to Produce.

2. You are requested to provide complete answers to this Request to produce, incorporating all information and knowledge within the possession of, or otherwise available to, you and your agents. If you are unable to answer any part of this Request to Produce in full, please answer to the extent possible, specify the reason for the inability to answer the remainder, set forth whatever information or knowledge is available concerning the unanswered portion, and identify all persons possessing further knowledge to the unanswered portion.

3. If you withhold or claim that you are entitled to withhold any information regarding any communication or documents, please state:

A. The privilege claimed in withholding the information.

B. If the information is related to a communication:

i. The parties to the communication;

ii. The date of the communication; and

iii. The general matter of the communication.

C. If the information relates to a document:

i. The privilege claimed in withholding the document;

ii. The author (s) and address (es) of the document and each person to whom copies were furnished;

iii. The date of the document;

iv. The general subject matter of the document; and

v. The present custodian of the document and its location.

DOCUMENTS TO PRODUCE

1. Entire Federal and State Income Tax Returns for the last five (5) years whether the same be in your name individually or jointly with anyone else, in your possession or under your control, including W-2 forms.

2. Records reflecting gross income and net income received by you either directly or indirectly since January 1, 1988 to the present, as well as your employee earning records and pay stubs prepared by your employer for the last twelve (12) months and estimated tax returns filed for the current year.

3. Any and all financial statements prepared within the last five (5) years, in your possession or under your control, whether in your name individually or jointly with anyone else.

4. a. Any and all of the following matters which are in your possession or under your control, whether held individually or jointly with anyone else, or in which you have an interest, or any account in which you have the right to withdraw any funds, whether or not your name appears on said account, during the last two (2) years involving any financial institutions, including but not limited to the following accounts:

(1) Checking accounts
(2) Savings accounts
(3) Certificates of Deposit
(4) Money Market Funds
(5) Ready Cash Accounts
(6) Credit Union Accounts
(7) Any other similar accounts.

b. All records and documents involving the above accounts, including but not limited to the following:

(1) All monthly statements
(2) All deposit slips
(3) All withdrawal slips
(4) All canceled checks
(5) Check stubs and check registers
(6) All savings account books
(7) All Credit Union account books
(8) Copies of all Certificates of Deposit
(9) All other similar records

5. All records, including but not limited to statements and other documents involving any stock ownership in which you either individually or jointly with anyone else (including your spouse) have or had an interest in during the last two (2) years.

6. All Bonds of any description in your possession or under your control whether in your name individually or jointly with anyone else, for the last two (2) years.

7. Any Note or other securities either in your possession or under your control, whether in your name individually or jointly with anyone else, for the last two (2) years.

8. All records in regards to any security account in your possession or under your control, whether in your name individually or jointly with anyone else, for the last two (2) years.

9. All records in regards to any current outstanding obligations upon which you are individually or jointly liable with anyone else, in your possession or under your control, for the last two (2) years.

10. A completed Financial Affidavit as attached.

11. All cashier's checks, money orders, or certified checks, in your possession or under your control, whether in your name individually or jointly with anyone else.

12. All life insurance policies.

13. All medical, hospitalization and dental policies.

14. All receipts, records of payment, bills, invoices, checks evidencing payment, as well as any other documents, correspondence or memorandums in your possession or under your control involving all credit cards which you might have used within the last year, whether or not the specific charges were authorized or signed by you or by any other party, including but not limited to the following: Visa, American Express, MasterCard, Diner's Club, all gasoline credit cards, and all department store credit cards.

15. All records and documents in regards to any 401 account, retirement fund, trust fund, profit sharing plan, pension plan, IRA account, KEOGH plan, or any other similar plan involving you, including but not limited to the following documents:

a. A copy of all of the plan and trust documents with all amendments, modifications and changes.

b. Copies of 5500/500-C, 500-B and 5500-SSA, if applicable, for the past three (3) years.

c. Copy of the trust asset statement as of the most recent plan anniversary.

d. Copy of the most recent Summary Plan Description.

e. If there are individual insurance or annuity contracts in force in the plan, a copy of the actual contracts.

f. If this is a profit sharing or defined contribution plan, a copy of the record of the individual account balance as of the last valuation date.

g. If there have been any loans made from the plan, a copy of the Note signed in support of the loan.

16. All records in regards to any real property, either owned or leased, either individually or jointly with anyone else, during the last five (5) years, including the Deed or an accurate copy of the same, all Closing Statements in regards to the purchase or sale of said property and all copies of any Notes and/or Mortgages, as well as all records in regards to any real property during the last three (3) years in which you were involved in the purchase in any way that was placed in someone else's name. Also, all records and other documents of any appraisals or evaluations of any of the above real property, including any appraisals done for ad valorem tax purposes by any governmental body.

17. All records of any person (including but not limited to a detective) who had your spouse or any other person who is or might be involved in this lawsuit under surveillance at any time during your marriage, together with their names, addresses, and telephone numbers. Further, any and all written documents, including reports or memoranda or documentary evidence of any kind, together with a list of the names and addresses of the persons who have possession of the same. Further, any movies, video tapes, and/or recordings of any sort, involving your spouse or any other person who is or might be involved in this lawsuit, taken at any time during your marriage, along with the necessary equipment to listen to or observe or watch the same.

18. All records in regards to any deferred income, deferred salary, and/or deferred commissions.

19. Personal property tax returns (intangible) for the last three (3) years.

20. Personal property tax returns (tangible) for the last three (3) years.

21. The most recent Real Estate Tax Notice indicating the assessed values for tax purposes of any and all real property held by you either individually, jointly with any other person or entity, or under your control.

22. Documents of title including Bills of Sale for all personal property, owned individually or with other persons, including automobiles, boats, airplanes, furniture, antiques, stamps and coin collections, during the current years and the past five (5) years.

23. All records, inventories and particularly any appraisals of any collections, such as but not limited to coin

collections, stamp collections, gem collections, antiques, gun collections or other similar collections.

24. All records, inventories and particularly any appraisals of any gold or silver in your possession or under your control, whether the same be held in your name individually or jointly with anyone else.

25. Schedule of all personal furniture, fixtures, furnishings and equipment owned individually or jointly during the current year and past five (5) years.

26. All records, including notes, mortgages or any other evidence of any security or collateral, in regards to any obligations which are owing to you either individually or jointly with any person, firm or corporation.

27. Any Trust, along with any amendments and modifications thereto, in which you individually or jointly with anyone else have an interest or in which you are a Beneficiary, Trustee, or Trustor, along with the most up-to-date financial records in regards to said Trust, amendments and modifications thereto, which list the assets, liabilities and income.

28. All of the following records in regards to any Trust in which you individually or jointly with anyone else have an interest or in which you are a Beneficiary, Trustee, or Trustor, to wit:

a. Records of all accounts in any financial institutions, money market funds, ready cash account, or other similar accounts, including monthly statements, deposit slips, withdrawal slips, canceled checks, savings accounts, certificates of deposit, and all other similar records for the last three years.

b. All financial statements, all annual accountings, all lists of inventories of assets, and Federal and State tax returns involving said Trust for the last three (3) years.

29. Any and all charts, graphs, records, documents, ledgers, drawings, or any other similar items, which have either been prepared by you or prepared by someone else, that you have in your possession or under your control, involving any of the issues involved in this action, including but not limited to any such items indicating he amount of personal expenses or costs incurred by you or your spouse, during the last five (5) years.

30. All records and documents in regards to any disability pension or other income or any other similar plan involving you, including but not limited to the following documents:

a. A copy of all of the plan and trust documents with all amendments, modifications and changes.

b. A copy of all documents which you initially signed, as well as any similar documents or amendments thereto involving any disability plan or income.

c. If there are individual insurance or annuity contracts in force in the plan, a copy of the actual contracts.

d. A copy of the most recent account balances as of the last valuation date.

e. If there have been any loans made from the plan, a copy of all documents, including Notes signed in support of the loan.

f. If you have cashed in, or received any lump sum payment, or any other similar type action involving any disability plan or income, a copy of all documents relating to the same.

g. A copy of all documents indicating whether you did or did not elect to provide survivor's benefits to any person, as well as any amendments thereto.

h. All documents evidencing your rights in regards to providing survivor benefits.

31. A copy of all Powers of Attorney or similar instruments involving you or your spouse and any recision, amendments or cancellation of the same.

32. A list setting forth the names and addresses of all persons who were witnesses to or have knowledge or information of any relevant facts relating to this action or who possess proof of the incidents or acts involved, their relationship to

you and indicating which were eyewitnesses; all written memoranda and reports and photographs submitted to you or your attorney by any such person; and all tape recordings or other evidence prepared from tape recordings made in connection with any wiretapping or other electronic surveillance conducted by you or others on your behalf.

33. A list of the names and addresses of all proposed expert witnesses and copies of all written reports rendered to you or your attorney by any such proposed expert witnesses.

34. Copies of all records concerning any safe deposit box used or maintained by the husband or wife during the current year and the past five (5) years, and all records of the contents of such box(es).

35. Records pertaining to any gifts received by you or your spouse during the marriage (limit to gifts with a value of $1000 or more).

36. Records pertaining to any inheritance received by you or your spouse during the marriage.

37. Any appraisal made within the last three (3) years.

It is requested that the aforesaid production be made on or before twenty eight (28) days from the date of service hereof, at the offices of ___________________________________.

Inspection will be made by visual observation and/or copying.

CHAPTER 11 PREPARING FOR A DIVORCE

The worst marriage is often better than the best divorce and every effort to preserve the marriage must be taken, especially for the children's sake. However, if you anticipate your wife is going to file against you, you should take the protective measures below. You can always give something back; at least you have control of the assets.

CHECKLIST

1. Cancel all credit cards.________

2. Clean out all bank and investment accounts.________

3. Collect all bank statements, utility bills, deeds, canceled checks, insurance policies and anything in the house that bears a dollar sign and deliver them to your attorney.

4. Pack a bag and keep it elsewhere This might even include some foodstuffs.

5. Contact an attorney experienced in custody cases who has a reputation as a fighter.

6. Become or remain deeply involved in your children's school activities. Meet with teachers, attend PTA meetings, ball games, etc.

7. Provide all the child care functions for your child.
   Homework______
   Diapers _____
   Meals__________
   Buy clothes_________
   Wash clothes_____

8. Make home movies of you and the child together.______

9. Make a Witness List of people who have observed you doing all the above________

10. At the last minute before anything is filed, clean out ALL valuables, guns, jewelry, personal effects, photos that mean a lot to you, etc. from the house and put in storage. Deny her anything to hock to pay for attorney fees and deny her control of anything she can hold over your head. Assume that whatever you leave in the house will never be seen again. Do this even if you NOW have control of the house.

D. ILLINOIS MENTAL CRUELTY STATUTE

§ 750 ILCS 5/401. Dissolution of marriage. Sec. 401. Dissolution of marriage.
(a) The court shall enter a judgment of dissolution of marriage if at the time the action was commenced one of the spouses was a resident of this state or was stationed in this state while a member of the armed services, and the residence or military presence had been maintained for 90 days next preceding the commencement of the action or the making of the finding; provided, however, that a finding of residence of a party in any judgment entered under this Act from January 1, 1982 through June 30, 1982 shall satisfy the former domicile requirements of this Act; and if one of the following grounds for dissolution has been proved:

(1) That, without cause or provocation by the petitioner: the respondent was at the time of such marriage, and continues to be, naturally impotent; the respondent had a wife or husband living at the time of the marriage; the respondent had committed adultery subsequent to the marriage; the respondent has wilfully deserted or absented himself or herself from the petitioner for the space of one year, including any period during which litigation may have pended between the spouses for dissolution of marriage or legal separation; the respondent has been guilty of habitual drunkenness for the space of 2 years; the respondent has been guilty of gross and confirmed habits caused by the excessive use of addictive drugs for the space of 2 years, or has attempted the life of the other by poison or other means showing malice, or has been guilty of extreme and repeated physical or mental cruelty, or has been convicted of a felony or other infamous crime; or the respondent has infected the other with a sexually transmitted disease. "Excessive use of addictive drugs", as used in this Section, refers to use of an addictive drug by a person when using the drug becomes a controlling or a dominant purpose of his life;

E. ILLINOIS IRRECONCILABLE DIFFERENCES STATUTE

§ 750 ILCS 5/401. Dissolution of marriage.

(2) That the spouses have lived separate and apart for a continuous period in excess of 2 years and irreconcilable differences have caused the irretrievable breakdown of the marriage and the court determines that efforts at reconciliation have failed or that future attempts at reconciliation would be impracticable and not in the best interests of the family. If the spouses have lived separate and apart for a continuous period of not less than 6 months next preceding the entry of the judgment dissolving the marriage, as evidenced by testimony or affidavits of the spouses, the requirement of living separate and apart for a continuous period in excess of 2 years may be waived upon written stipulation of both spouses filed with the court. At any time after the parties cease to cohabit, the following periods shall be included in the period of separation:

(A) any period of cohabitation during which the parties attempted in good faith to reconcile and participated in marriage counseling under the guidance of any of the following: a psychiatrist, a clinical psychologist, a clinical social worker, a marriage and family therapist, a person authorized to provide counseling in accordance with the prescriptions of any religious denomination, or a person regularly engaged in providing family or marriage counseling; and

(B) any period of cohabitation under written agreement of the parties to attempt to reconcile. In computing the period during which the spouses have lived separate and apart for purposes of this Section, periods during which the spouses were living separate and apart prior to July 1, 1984 are included.

F. ILLINOIS MAXIMUM INVOLVEMENT PRESUMPTION

§ 750 ILCS 5/602.
Sec. 602. Best Interest of Child.
(a) The court shall determine custody in accordance with the best interest of the child. The court shall consider all relevant factors including....

(c) Unless the court finds the occurrence of ongoing abuse as defined in Section 103 of the Illinois Domestic Violence Act of 1986 [750 ILCS 60/103], **the court shall presume that the maximum involvement and cooperation of both parents** regarding the physical, mental, moral, and emotional well-being of their child **is in the best interest of the child**. There shall be no presumption in favor of or against joint custody. (*see page 164 for whole text*)

G. ILLINOIS PROPERTY STATUTES

§ 750 ILCS 5/503. Disposition of property.
Sec. 503. Disposition of property.
(a) For purposes of this Act, "marital property" means all property acquired by either spouse subsequent to the marriage, except the following, which is known as "non-marital property:"

(1) property acquired by gift, legacy or descent;
(2) property acquired in exchange for property acquired before the marriage or in exchange for property acquired by gift, legacy or descent;
(3) property acquired by a spouse after a judgment of legal separation;
(4) property excluded by valid agreement of the parties;
(5) any judgment or property obtained by judgment awarded to a spouse from the other spouse;
(6) property acquired before the marriage;
(7) the increase in value of property acquired by a method listed in paragraphs (1) through (6) of this subsection, irrespective of whether the increase results from a contribution of marital property, non-marital property, the personal effort of a spouse, or otherwise, subject to the right of reimbursement provided in subsection (c) of this Section; and
(8) income from property acquired by a method listed in paragraphs (1) through (7) of this subsection if the income is not attributable to the personal effort of a spouse.

(b) For purposes of distribution of property pursuant to this Section, all property acquired by either spouse after the marriage and before a judgment of dissolution of marriage or declaration of invalidity of marriage, including non-marital property transferred into some form of co-ownership between the spouses, is presumed to be marital property, regardless of whether title is held individually or by the spouses in some form of co-ownership such as joint tenancy, tenancy in common, tenancy by the entirety, or community property. The presumption of marital property is overcome by a showing that the property was acquired by a method listed in subsection (a) of this Section.

(c) Commingled marital and non-marital property shall be treated in the following manner, unless otherwise agreed by the spouses:

(1) When marital and non-marital property are commingled by contributing one estate of property into another resulting in a loss of identity of the contributed property, the classification of the contributed property is transmuted to the estate receiving the contribution, subject to the provisions of paragraph (2) of this subsection; provided that if marital and non-marital property are commingled into newly acquired property resulting in a loss of identity of the contributing

estates, the commingled property shall be deemed transmuted to marital property, subject to the provisions of paragraph (2) of this subsection.

(2) When one estate of property makes a contribution to another estate of property, or when a spouse contributes personal effort to non-marital property, the contributing estate shall be reimbursed from the estate receiving the contribution notwithstanding any transmutation; provided, that no such reimbursement shall be made with respect to a contribution which is not retraceable by clear and convincing evidence, or was a gift, or, in the case of a contribution of personal effort of a spouse to non-marital property, unless the effort is significant and results in substantial appreciation of the non-marital property. Personal effort of a spouse shall be deemed a contribution by the marital estate. The court may provide for reimbursement out of the marital property to be divided or by imposing a lien against the non-marital property which received the contribution.

(d) In a proceeding for dissolution of marriage or declaration of invalidity of marriage, or in a proceeding for disposition of property following dissolution of marriage by a court which lacked personal jurisdiction over the absent spouse or lacked jurisdiction to dispose of the property, the court shall assign each spouse's non-marital property to that spouse. It also shall divide the marital property without regard to marital misconduct in just proportions considering all relevant factors, including:

(1) the contribution of each party to the acquisition, preservation, or increase or decrease in value of the marital or non-marital property, including the contribution of a spouse as a homemaker or to the family unit;
(2) the dissipation by each party of the marital or non-marital property;
(3) the value of the property assigned to each spouse;
(4) the duration of the marriage;
(5) the relevant economic circumstances of each spouse when the division of property is to become effective, including the desirability of awarding the family home, or the right to live therein for reasonable periods, to the spouse having custody of the children;
(6) any obligations and rights arising from a prior marriage of either party;
(7) any antenuptial agreement of the parties;
(8) the age, health, station, occupation, amount and sources of income, vocational skills, employability, estate, liabilities, and needs of each of the parties;
(9) the custodial provisions for any children;
(10) whether the apportionment is in lieu of or in addition to maintenance;
(11) the reasonable opportunity of each spouse for future acquisition of capital assets and income; and
(12) the tax consequences of the property division upon the respective economic circumstances of the parties.

(e) Each spouse has a species of common ownership in the marital property which vests at the time dissolution proceedings are commenced and continues only during the pendency of the action. Any such interest in marital property shall not encumber that property so as to restrict its transfer, assignment or conveyance by the title holder unless such title holder is specifically enjoined from making such transfer, assignment or conveyance.

(f) In a proceeding for dissolution of marriage or declaration of invalidity of marriage or in a proceeding for disposition of property following dissolution of marriage by a court that lacked personal jurisdiction over the absent spouse or lacked jurisdiction to dispose of the property, the court, in determining the value of the marital and non-marital property for purposes of dividing the property, shall value the property as of the date of trial or some other date as close to the date of trial as is practicable.

(g) The court if necessary to protect and promote the best interests of the children may set aside a portion of the jointly or separately held estates of the parties in a separate fund or trust for the support, maintenance, education, and general welfare of any minor, dependent, or incompetent child of the parties. In making a determination under this subsection, the court may consider, among other things, the conviction of a party of any of the offenses set forth in Section 12-4, 12- 4.1, 12-4.2, 12-4.3, 12-13, 12-14, 12-14.1, 12-15, or 12-16 of the Criminal Code of 1961 [720 ILCS 5/12-4, 720 ILCS 5/12-4.1, 720 ILCS 5/12-4.2, 720 ILCS 5/12-4.3, 720 ILCS 5/12-13, 720 ILCS 5/12-14, 720 ILCS 5/12-14.1, 720 ILCS 5/12-15, or 720 ILCS 5/12-16] if the victim is a child of one or both of the parties, and there is a need for, and cost of, care, healing and counseling for the child who is the victim of the crime.

(h) Unless specifically directed by a reviewing court, or upon good cause shown, the court shall not on remand consider any increase or decrease in the value of any "marital" or "non-marital" property occurring since the assessment of such property at the original trial or hearing, but shall use only that assessment made at the original trial or hearing.

(i) The court may make such judgments affecting the marital property as may be just and may enforce such judgments by ordering a sale of marital property, with proceeds therefrom to be applied as determined by the court.

H. **COUNTER-PETITION FOR CUSTODY**

IN THE CIRCUIT COURT
OF THE _FIRST JUDICIAL CIRCUIT
JACKSON COUNTY, ILLINOIS

IN RE THE MARRIAGE OF	)	
	)	
__________________,	)	
Plaintiff/Counter-Defendant,	)	
	)	Case No.
v.	)	
	)	
__________________,	)	
Defendant/Counter-Plaintiff.	)	

COUNTER-PETITION FOR CUSTODY

NOW COMES the Defendant/Counter-Plaintiff,_________________, by and through his attorney, _______________, and for his Counter-Petition for Custody, alleges as follows:

1. Defendant/Counter-Plaintiff, is __ years of age, is employed as a _____________, and has resided in ________, _____ County, Illinois, for more than ninety days next preceding the filing of this Petition.

2. Plaintiff/Counter-Defendant, _________________ is __ years of age, is employed as a _________________, and has resided in ________, _____ County, Illinois, for more than ninety days next preceding the filing of this Petition.

3. The parties were married on ________, ____. The marriage was registered in _____ County, Illinois.

4. One child was born to the parties of the marriage, namely: _______________, born _______________, age __. No children have been adopted by the parties and the wife is not now pregnant.

5. It is in the best interests of the minor child that her permanent care, custody, control and education be awarded solely to Defendant/Counter-Plaintiff.

6. Plaintiff/Counter-Defendant is able-bodied and intelligent and capable of contributing to the financial support of the minor child and should be required to contribute in such sums as the Court deems just and in accordance with statutes provided.

WHEREFORE, Defendant/Counter-Plaintiff,_________________, respectfully prays as follows:

A. For an Order awarding the permanent care, custody, control and education of the minor child to Defendant/Counter-Plaintiff.

B. For an Order requiring Plaintiff/Counter-Defendant to contribute to the financial support of the minor child.

C. For such other and further relief as this Court deems just and equitable.

_______________________________________,
Defendant/Counter-Plaintiff

_______________________________________,
Attorney for Defendant/Counter-Plaintiff

VERIFICATION

Under penalties as provided by law pursuant to Section 1-109 of the Code of Civil Procedure, the undersigned certifies that the statements set forth in this instrument are true and correct, except as to matters therein stated to be on information and belief and as to such matters the undersigned certifies as aforesaid that he verily believes the same to be true.

_______________________________________,
Defendant/Counter-Plaintiff

PROOF OF SERVICE

The undersigned certifies that a copy of the foregoing instrument, Counter-Petition for Custody, was served upon:

by enclosing the same in an envelope addressed as shown above, with postage fully prepaid and by depositing said envelope in a U.S. Post Office mailbox in Carbondale, Illinois, on the _____ day of _______, 2000.

____

SAMPLE HOURLY FEE AGREEMENT FOR LEGAL SERVICES

AGREEMENT FOR LEGAL SERVICES

(Hourly Fee)
_______________, Attorney at Law

This contract for legal services is made between _______________, Attorney at Law, hereinafter called "attorney," and _________________________, hereinafter called "client."

In consideration of the following covenants and conditions, it is mutually agreed as follows:

1. Client hereby retains and employs the attorney for representation with regard to the following matters:

a. The prosecution of a claim against _________________________________ arising out of an occurrence on or about ___________________________.

2. In consideration for availability of attorney and services rendered and to be rendered, client agrees to pay attorney in accordance with the sub paragraphs below:

a. The sum of ___________ as a non-refundable retainer to be credited toward the client's hourly charges.(some states including Illinois have barred non refundable retainers and require a standard disclosure form)

b. Hourly charges at the rate of $150.00 per hour.

c. The retainer is not a fixed fee and if exceeded will result in weekly billing for hours expended.

3. Client agrees that in addition to the above attorney's fees, all costs and expenses incurred in the investigation of this matter shall be paid by the client. The term "costs" shall include, but is not limited to, court costs, subpoena costs, photographs, depositions and court reporter costs, reports, witness statements, expenses incurred in investigating, handling, or litigating this claim, including long distance telephone calls, postage, and xerox.

4. In the event of client's death, attorney's fees, costs and expenses owed under this agreement shall have first priority as a first class claim against client's estate in addition to all other remedies provided by law.

5. Client agrees to pay all attorney's fees ordered by the Court as sanctions imposed under Illinois Supreme Court Rule 137 against client or attorney. Client agrees to fully and truthfully disclose the facts of his case to attorney prior to filing any legal action.

6. Client agrees to pay all bills within ten (10) days after weekly billing. Statements for services rendered which are delinquent more than thirty (30) days are subject to an 18% per annum interest charge. In the event of default in payment as provided above, client will pay reasonable attorney's fees and costs incurred in collecting the amount due and owing attorneys.

7. Client agrees that time is of the essence and failure to make payments of legal fees or costs and expenses as described in #3 above within ten (10) days after billing shall entitle attorney to Petition to Withdraw from client's case. Client agrees that prior to any hearing, legal fees must be paid up to date and prior to any final hearing, sufficient funds to cover the cost of the final hearing must be on deposit in the retainer trust account. Attorney shall have no obligation to participate in any final hearing for which funds are not on deposit.

Signed this _________ day of _____________, 2000.

CLIENT: ____________________________

WITNESS: ___________________________

I hereby agree to accept professional responsibility for the matter entrusted to me and to make no settlement without the consent of my client.

____

Attorney for Client

CHAPTER 12 FATHERS' RIGHTS INTERNET LEGAL RESOURCES

If you're going to fight for Father's Rights, you need the most modern effective tools and a communications network.. Gain access to the Internet and on-line services. A wealth of information and assistance is available. Some valuable resources are listed later in this book.

Boards: alt.support divorce and alt.support dadsrights are worth checking out.

THE INTERNET (or World Wide Web, WWW)- some useful addresses.

- **fathers-rights.com**
- dadslawyer.com.
- lowersupport.com
- fathersrights.org
- Law Links - http://www.Counsel.com:80/
  American Information Network - http://www.vix.com/men/org/track.html
- Legal Sights - http://www.rbvdnr.com/legals.html (links)
- University of Illinois Law Library - http://www.law.uiuc.edu/uilaw/library/library.html
- Promoting Responsible fatherhood(**SWISS/European**)
  Verantwotungsvoll erziehende Vaeter - http://www.vev.ch/

APPENDIX

ILLINOIS STATUTES (TYPICAL)

CRIMINAL CODE
§ 720 ILCS 5/10-5.5. Unlawful visitation interference

Sec. 10-5.5. Unlawful visitation interference.

(a) As used in this Section, the terms "child", "detain," and "lawful custodian" shall have the meanings ascribed to them in Section 10-5 of this Code [720 ILCS 5/10-5].

(b) Every person who, in violation of the visitation provisions of a court order relating to child custody, detains or conceals a child with the intent to deprive another person of his or her rights to visitation shall be guilty of unlawful visitation interference.

(c) A person committing unlawful visitation interference is guilty of a petty offense. However, any person violating this Section after 2 prior convictions of unlawful visitation interference is guilty of a Class A misdemeanor.

(d) Any law enforcement officer who has probable cause to believe that a person has committed or is committing an act in violation of this Section shall issue to that person a notice to appear.

(e) The notice shall:

(1) be in writing;

(2) state the name of the person and his address, if known

(3) set forth the nature of the offense;

(4) be signed by the officer issuing the notice; and

(5) request the person to appear before a court at a certain time and place.

(f) Upon failure of the person to appear, a summons or warrant of arrest may be issued.

(g) It is an affirmative defense that:

(1) a person or lawful custodian committed the act to protect the child from imminent physical harm, provided that the defendant's belief that there was physical harm imminent was reasonable and that the defendant's conduct in withholding visitation rights was a reasonable response to the harm believed imminent;

(2) the act was committed with the mutual consent of all parties having a right to custody and visitation of the child; or

(3) the act was otherwise authorized by law.

(h) A person convicted of unlawful visitation interference shall not be subject to a civil contempt citation for the same conduct for violating visitation provisions of a court order issued under the Illinois Marriage and Dissolution of Marriage Act [750 ILCS 5/101 et seq.]. **§ 750 ILCS 5/102. Purposes; Rules of Construction of the Illinois Marriage and Dissolution of Marriage Act:**

Sec. 102. Purposes; Rules of Construction. This Act shall be liberally construed and applied to promote its underlying purposes, which are to:

(1) provide adequate procedures for the solemnization and registration of marriage;

(2) strengthen and preserve the integrity of marriage and safeguard family relationships;

(3) promote the amicable settlement of disputes that have arisen between parties to a marriage;

(4) mitigate the potential harm to the spouses and their children caused by the process of legal dissolution of marriage;

(5) make reasonable provision for spouses and minor children during and after litigation;

(6) eliminate the consideration of marital misconduct in the adjudication of rights and duties incident to the legal dissolution of marriage, legal separation and declaration of invalidity of marriage;

(7) secure the **maximum involvement and cooperation of both parents** regarding the physical, mental, moral and emotional well-being of the children during and after the litigation.

§ 750 ILCS 5/602. Best Interest of Child

Sec. 602. Best Interest of Child.

(a) The court shall determine custody in accordance with the best interest of the child. The court shall consider all relevant factors including:

(1) the wishes of the child's parent or parents as to his custody;
(2) the wishes of the child as to his custodian;
(3) the interaction and interrelationship of the child with his parent or parents, his siblings and any other person who may significantly affect the child's best interest;
(4) the child's adjustment to his home, school and community;
(5) the mental and physical health of all individuals involved;
(6) the physical violence or threat of physical violence by the child's potential custodian, whether directed against the child or directed against another person;
(7) the occurrence of ongoing abuse as defined in Section 103 of the Illinois Domestic Violence Act of 1986 [750 ILCS 60/103], whether directed against the child or directed against another person; and
(8) the willingness and ability of each parent to facilitate and encourage a close and continuing relationship between the other parent and the child. (This wins custody!)

(b) The court shall not consider conduct of a present or proposed custodian that does not affect his relationship to the child.

(c) Unless the court finds the occurrence of ongoing abuse as defined in Section 103 of the Illinois Domestic Violence Act of 1986 [750 ILCS 60/103], the court shall presume that the maximum involvement and cooperation of both parents regarding the physical, mental, moral, and emotional well-being of their child is in the best interest of the child. There shall be no presumption in favor of or against joint custody.

§ 750 ILCS 5/505. Child support; contempt; penalties.

Sec. 505. Child support; contempt; penalties.

(a) In a proceeding for dissolution of marriage, legal separation, declaration of invalidity of marriage, a proceeding for child support following dissolution of the marriage by a court which lacked personal jurisdiction over the absent spouse, a proceeding for modification of a previous order for child support under Section 510 of this Act [750 ILCS 5/510], or any proceeding authorized under Section 501 or 601 of this Act [750 ILCS 5/501 or 750 ILCS 5/601], the court may order either or both parents owing a duty of support to a child of the marriage to pay an amount reasonable and necessary for his support, without regard to marital misconduct. The duty of support owed to a minor child includes the obligation to provide for the reasonable and necessary physical, mental and emotional health needs of the child.

(1) The Court shall determine the minimum amount of support by using the following guidelines:

Number of Children	Percent of Supporting Party's Net Income
1	20%
2	28%
3	32%
4	40%
5	45%
6 or more	50%

(2) The above guidelines shall be applied in each case unless the court makes a finding that the application of the guidelines would be inappropriate, after considering the best interests of the child in light of evidence including but not limited to one or more of the following relevant factors:

(a) the financial resources of the child;

(b) the financial resources and needs of the custodial parent;

(c) the standard of living the child would have enjoyed had the marriage not been dissolved;

(d) the physical and emotional condition of the child, and his educational needs; and

(e) the financial resources and needs of the non-custodial parent. If the court deviates from the guidelines, the court's finding shall state the amount of support that would have been required under the guidelines, if determinable. The court shall include the reason or reasons for the variance from the guidelines. (3) "Net income" is defined as the total of all income from all sources, minus the following deductions:

(a) Federal income tax (properly calculated withholding or estimated payments);

(b) State income tax (properly calculated withholding or estimated payments);

(c) Social Security (FICA payments);

(d) Mandatory retirement contributions required by law or as a condition of employment;

(e) Union dues;

(f) Dependent and individual health/hospitalization insurance premiums;

(g) Prior obligations of support or maintenance actually paid pursuant to a court order;

(h) Expenditures for repayment of debts that represent reasonable and necessary expenses for the production of income, medical expenditures necessary to preserve life or health, reasonable expenditures for the benefit of the child and the other parent, exclusive of gifts. The court shall reduce net income in determining the minimum amount of support to be ordered only for the period that such payments are due and shall enter an order containing provisions for its self-executing modification upon termination of such payment period.

(4) In cases where the court order provides for health/hospitalization insurance coverage pursuant to Section 505.2 of this Act [750 ILCS 5/505.2], the premiums for that insurance, or that portion of the premiums for which the supporting party is responsible in the case of insurance provided through an employer's health insurance plan where the employer pays a portion of the premiums, shall be subtracted from net income in determining the minimum amount of support to be ordered.

(4.5) In a proceeding for child support following dissolution of the marriage by a court that lacked personal jurisdiction over the absent spouse, and in which the court is requiring payment of support for the period before the date an order for current support is entered, there is a rebuttable presumption that the supporting party's net income for the prior period was the same as his or her net income at the time the order for current support is entered.

(5) If the net income cannot be determined because of default or any other reason, the court shall order support in an amount considered reasonable in the particular case. The final order in all cases shall state the support level in dollar amounts.

(b) Failure of either parent to comply with an order to pay support shall be punishable as in other cases of contempt. In addition to other penalties provided by law the Court may, after finding the parent guilty of contempt, order that the parent be:

(1) placed on probation with such conditions of probation as the Court deems advisable;

(2) sentenced to periodic imprisonment for a period not to exceed 6 months; provided, however, that the Court may permit the parent to be released for periods of time during the day or night to:

(A) work; or

(B) conduct a business or other self-employed occupation. The Court may further order any part or all of the earnings of a parent during a sentence of periodic imprisonment paid to the Clerk of the Circuit Court or to the parent having custody or to the guardian having custody of the minor children of the sentenced parent for the support of said minor children until further order of the Court.

(c) A one-time charge of 20% is imposable upon the amount of past-due child support owed on July 1, 1988 which has accrued under a support order entered by the court. The charge shall be imposed in accordance with the provisions of Section 10-21 of the Illinois Public Aid Code [305 ILCS 5/10-21] and shall be enforced by the court upon petition.

(d) Any new or existing support order entered by the court under this Section shall be deemed to be a series of judgments against the person obligated to pay support thereunder, each such judgment to be in the amount of each payment or installment of support and each such judgment to be deemed entered as of the date the corresponding payment or installment becomes due under the terms of the support order. Each such judgment shall have the full force, effect and attributes of any other judgment of this State, including the ability to be enforced.

(e) When child support is to be paid through the clerk of the court in a county of 1,000,000 inhabitants or less, the order shall direct the obligor to pay to the clerk, in addition to the child support payments, all fees imposed by the county board under paragraph (3) of subsection (u) of Section 27.1 of the Clerks of Courts Act [705 ILCS 105/27.1]. Unless paid in cash or pursuant to an order for withholding, the payment of the fee shall be by a separate instrument from the support payment and shall be made to the order of the Clerk.

(f) An order for support entered or modified in a case in which a party is receiving child and spouse support services under Article X of the Illinois Public Aid Code [305 ILCS 5/10-1 et seq.] shall include a provision requiring the obligor to notify the Illinois Department of Public Aid, within 7 days, 1(i) of the name and address of any new employer of the obligor, (ii) whether the obligor has access to health insurance coverage through the employer or other group coverage, and (iii) if so, the policy name and number and the names of persons covered under the policy.

(g) An order for support shall include a date on which the current support obligation terminates. The termination date shall be no earlier than the date on which the child covered by the order will attain the age of majority or is otherwise emancipated. The order for support shall state that the termination date does not apply to any arrearage that may remain unpaid on that date. Nothing in this subsection shall be construed to prevent the court from modifying the order.

§ 750 ILCS 5/505.1. [Unemployed obligor; powers of court].

Sec. 505.1. Whenever it is determined in a proceeding to establish or enforce a child support or maintenance obligation that the person owing a duty of support is unemployed, the court may order the person to seek employment and report periodically to the court with a diary, listing or other memorandum of his or her efforts in accordance with such order. Additionally, the court may order the unemployed person to report to the Department of Employment Security for job search services or to make application with the local Jobs Training Partnership Act provider for participation in job search, training or work programs and where the duty of support is owed to a child receiving support services under Article X of The Illinois Public Aid Code, as amended [305 ILCS 5/10-1 et seq.], the court may order the unemployed person to report to the Illinois Department of Public Aid for participation in job search, training or work programs established under Section 9-6 of that Code [305 ILCS 5/9-6].

§ 750 ILCS 5/508. Attorney's Fees.

Illinois Marriage and Dissolution of Marriage Act

Sec. 508. Attorney's Fees.

(a) The court from time to time, after due notice and hearing, and after considering the financial resources of the parties, may order any party to pay a reasonable amount for his own costs and attorney's fees and for the costs and attorney's fees necessarily incurred or, for the purpose of enabling a party lacking sufficient financial resources to obtain or retain legal representation, expected to be incurred by any party, which award shall be made in connection with the following:

(1) The maintenance or defense of any proceeding under this Act.

(2) The enforcement or modification of any order or judgment under this Act.

(3) The defense of an appeal of any order or judgment under this Act, including the defense of appeals of post-judgment orders.

(4) The maintenance or defense of a petition brought under Section 2-1401 of the Code of Civil Procedure [735 ILCS 5/2-1401] seeking relief from a final order or judgment under this Act.

(5) The costs and legal services of an attorney rendered in preparation of the commencement of the proceeding brought under this act

(b) In every proceeding for the enforcement of an order or judgment when the court finds that the failure to comply with the order or judgment was without cause or justification, the court shall order the party against whom the proceeding is brought to pay the costs and reasonable attorney's fees of the prevailing party.

(c) The court may order that the award of attorney's fees and costs hereunder shall be paid directly to the attorney, who may enforce such order in his name, or that they be paid to the relevant party. Judgment may be entered and enforcement thereof had accordingly.

CAUTION

Recent laws attempt to level the field of litigation by requiring payment of interim attorney fees equal to fees you have paid your attorney! Discuss this with your attorney. You may want your MOM to pay your attorney fees on her mastercard, only of course if you can't pay them yourself! If you have a large amount of disposable cash PAY OFF DEBTS so you don't risk being stuck with them!.

PLEADINGS TO FIGHT FOR CUSTODY

IN THE CIRCUIT COURT OF THE (Circuit Number) JUDICIAL CIRCUIT
(County) COUNTY, ILLINOIS

In Re: The Marriage of:	)	
	)	
(YOU),	)	
	)	
Petitioner,	)	
	)	CASE NO : (Case and number)
	)	
(YOUR EX),	)	
	)	
Respondent.	)	

PETITION FOR DISSOLUTION OF MARRIAGE

NOW COMES the Petitioner, (Your Name), individually and by his attorney, (Your Attorney), pursuant to the Illinois Marriage and Dissolution Act, and asks this court to dissolve his marriage to the Respondent (Your ex's LEGAL name). In support of his Petition, he alleges:

1. This Court has Jurisdiction over the parties:
(a) (Your Name) resides at (YOUR ADDRESS), (YOUR APT. #), (YOUR CITY, STATE, ZIP) and
(b) (Your ex's LEGAL name) resides at (YOUR EX'S STREET ADDRESS), (YOUR EX'S CITY, STATE, ZIP).

2. (Your Name) and (Your ex's LEGAL name) were married on (when you married) at (where you married), and their marriage was registered in ____________.

3. (Your Name) is employed at (your employer).

4. (Your ex's LEGAL name) is employed at (your ex's job).

5. (Your children with ex ONLY) children were born to the parties as a result of this marriage, namely: (child A's name), born (child A's b-date), (child B's name), born (child B's b-date), (child C's name), born (child C's b--date) and (child D's name), born (child D's b-date). No other children were born to or adopted by the parties and the Wife is not now pregnant.

6. That without cause and provocation of the part of Petitioner, the Respondent has been guilty of extreme and repeated acts of mental cruelty.

7. That (Your Name) is a fit and proper person to have sole care, custody, control and education of the minor child(ren) of the parties.

8. It is in the best interest of said minor child(ren) that (Your Name) be awarded custody with (Your ex's LEGAL name) receiving reasonable and liberal visitation.

9. That the parties have acquired certain real property which requires disposition by the Court.

10. That the parties have acquired certain items of personal property requiring disposition by the Court.

11. That the parties have acquired certain marital debts requiring disposition by the Court.

12. That the Respondent is well able to support herself and should be barred from receiving maintenance from (Your Name).

WHEREFORE, the Petitioner respectfully prays that:

1. Enter a Judgment of Dissolution of marriage in favor of both parties dissolving their marriage.

2. Award (Your Name) sole care, custody, control and education of his minor child(ren), namely: (child A's name), (child B's name), (child C's name), and (child D's name).

3. That (Your Name) be awarded as his sole and absolute property all his non-marital property.

5. That the Marital property be equitably distributed.

6. That the marital debts be equitably allocated.

7. That (Your ex's LEGAL name) be barred from past, present and future maintenance from (Your Name).

8. For such further relief the Court deems just and proper.

(Your Name)

BY______________

(Your Attorney)
Attorney at Law
(Your Attorney's Address)
(Your Attorney's City, State)
(Your Attorney's Phone)

VERIFICATION

Under penalties as provided by law pursuant to Section 1-109 of the Code of Civil Procedure, the undersigned certifies that the statements set forth in this instrument are true and correct, except as to matters therein stated to be on information and belief and as to such matters the undersigned certifies as aforesaid that he verily believes the same to be true.

____
(Your Name)

PROOF OF SERVICE

The undersigned certifies that a copy of the foregoing instrument was served upon:
(Your Ex's Attorney)
(Ex's Attorney's address)
(Ex's Attorney's Suite No.)
(Ex's Attorney's City, State, Zip)
by enclosing the same in an envelope addressed as shown above, with postage fully prepaid, and by depositing said envelope in a U.S. Post Office mailbox in Carbondale, Illinois, on the ____ day of ________________________, 2000.

____
(Your Attorney)

(Your Attorney)
(Your Attorney's Address)
(Your Attorney's City, State, Zip)
(Your Attorney's Phone)

STATE OF ILLINOIS
IN THE CIRCUIT COURT OF THE _ JUDICIAL CIRCUIT
_____COUNTY, ILLINOIS

IN RE THE MARRIAGE OF	)	
MARIE __________________	)	
	)	
Petitioner,	)	
v.	)	NO. 99-D-
ALFRED _________________,	)	
	)	
Respondent.	)	

PETITION FOR TEMPORARY CUSTODY AND CHILD SUPPORT

NOW COMES the Respondent, Alfred __________, by and through his attorney, RONALD L. ISAACS, and pursuant to 750 ILCS 5/501 and 603, respectfully prays this Court grant him certain temporary relief and in support of his Petition respectfully states as follows:

1. That Petitioner filed a Petition for Dissolution of Marriage on May 22, 1995.

2. There are two living minor children of the parties: ______________, born May 18, 1982 and __________________born ___________________.

3. That since May 22, 1995 until the filing of this Petition the minor children have lived with the Petitioner.

4. Respondent has made demands upon Petitioner for custody of his minor children and child support and temporary visitation and custody.

5. By reason of the Petitioner s unwillingness to consider the best interests of the minor children by denying visitation between Respondent and his children Petitioner has evidenced a total inability to foster a relationship between a non-custodial parent and his children and fails that test for custody under 735 ILCS 5/2

6. The children free of coercion from the Petitioner would wish to remain under the care, custody and control of the Respondent.

7. Respondent is the natural father of the children. Respondent has reared them since time of birth, and has provided for their physical, mental, spiritual and cultural needs, and is a fit and proper person to have sole custody, care, control and education of his minor children.

8. That Respondent will use his best efforts to enhance and encourage the respect, love and affection of the children toward each parent and will implement a relationship with the children that will give each child the maximum feeling of security that may be possible.

9. It is in the best interests of the children that Respondent be granted temporary sole custody, care and control of his two children, XXXXXX and XXXXXXXXXX and reasonable child support.

10. In support of this Petition the affidavit of the Respondent is attached and made a part of this document.

WHEREFORE, the Respondent respectfully requests this Honorable Court enter an Order as follows:

A. Granting him the temporary custody of the minor children of the parties, subject to the rights of visitation as are deemed reasonable and proper to be granted to the Petitioner.

B. That the Petitioner be ordered to pay such sums

as this Court deems reasonable and proper for the temporary support of the minor children of the parties.

C. That the Petitioner be Ordered to pay attorney fees and costs incurred by the Respondent.

D. For such other relief the Court deems just.

____

Ronald L. Isaacs,
Attorney for Respondent

STATE OF ILLINOIS)
) SS
COUNTY OF JACKSON)

Under penalties as provided by law pursuant to Section 1-109 of the Code of Civil Procedure, the undersigned certifies that the statements set forth in this instrument are true and correct, except as to matters therein stated to be on information and belief and as to such matters the undersigned certifies as aforesaid that he verily believes the same to be true.

______________________ ALFRED XXXXXXX.

Subscribed and sworn to before me this _____ day of _______________, 2000.

____
Notary Public

My Commission expires:

____

RONALD ISAACS
ATTORNEY AT LAW
10325 Winterhue Drive
Baton Rouge, LA 70810
(225) 757 0607

PROOF OF SERVICE

The undersigned certifies that a copy of the foregoing instrument was served upon the attorneys of record of all parties to the above cause by enclosing the same in an envelope addressed to such attorneys at their business address as disclosed by the pleadings of record herein, with postage fully prepaid and by depositing said envelope in the U.S. Post Office mail box in Carbondale, Illinois, on the _____ day of ____________________, 2000.

STATE OF ILLINOIS
IN THE CIRCUIT COURT OF THE __JUDICIAL CIRCUIT
__________ COUNTY, ILLINOIS

JUSTIN XXXXXXXXX)
)
Petitioner,)
) No.: 98-D-
LAURA XXXXXXXX)
)
Respondent.)

PETITION TO MODIFY JUDGEMENT OF DISSOLUTION OF MARRIAGE

Now comes the Plaintiff, XXXXXXX, by his attorney Ronald Isaacs and for his Petition states:

1. That the Judgement of Dissolution incorporated a marital settlement agreement between the parties.

2. That such marital settlement agreement provided in part as follows:

"A. Custody and Visitation:
The parties agree that Wife shall have the sole custody, control and education of the minor child, subject to visitation as follows: Husband shall have visitation with the minor child of the parties from May 30th of every year until August 1st of every year. The parties have been able to cooperate in the past about visitation and therefore no other specific visitation schedule is provided for weekly visitation. However, it is the intent of the parties and the past practice of the parties to allow Husband to have liberal visitation which Wife agrees to provide and encourage."

3. That such terms for visitation have become unworkable, unreasonable and not in the best interests of the minor child and a definite pickup place should be ordered and that petitioner should pickup the child for visitation and respondent should pickup the child after visitation.

4. The period of visitation from May 30th to August 1st of each year is too short and does not provide maximum involvement between the Plaintiff and his child. A longer continuous period would further the relationship between the child and Plaintiff, the non custodial parent.

5. That a specific visitation schedule is required because Defendant failed to provide reasonable visitation between the Plaintiff and his child. That Justin XXXXXX would propose the following visitation schedule:

a. Every other weekend from Friday at 5:00 p.m. to Sunday at 8:00 p.m.
b. Every Wednesday from 5:00 p.m. to 5:00 p.m. Thursday
c. Plaintiff would have overnight visitation on every Federal holiday from 8:00 p.m. the preceding night to 8:00 p.m. of the holiday.
d. That the childs birthday be alternated each year between parents from 8:00 p.m. the preceding evening to 8:00 p.m. of the birthday.
e. That Christmas Eve from 8:00 a.m. to 8:00 p.m. and Christmas Day (8:00 p.m.

Christmas Eve to 8:00 p.m. Christmas Day) be alternated between parents.

f. That Petitioner have the child from May 30th to August 30th each year with Defendant exercising visitation from 8:00 p.m. Friday to 8:00 p.m. Sunday one weekend each month.

g. That Petitioner have visitation in lieu of the child being left with a babysitter when Petitioner is available to babysit.

h. That child support be reduced by 2/3 from May 30th through August 30th.

Wherefore Plaintiff moves the Court modify its Judgement of Dissolution of Marriage and for such other relief the Court deems just.

____

Justin XXXXXXXXX

____

Ronald Isaacs

VERIFICATION

The undersigned, being first duly sworn on oath deposes and states that the contents of the foregoing document are true (except as to matter alleged to be on information and belief and those he believes to be true).

____

JUSTIN XXXXXX

Subscribed and sworn to before me this __________ day of October, 1999.

____

Notary Public

STATE OF ILLINOIS)
) SS.
COUNTY OF JACKSON)

AFFIDAVIT

I, XXXXXXXX, certify that I have read the foregoing document and that to the best of my knowledge, information, and belief formed after reasonable inquiry it is well grounded in fact and is warranted by existing law or a good faith argument for the extension, modification, or reversal of existing law and that it is not interposed for any improper purpose, such as to harass or to cause unnecessary delay or a needless increase in the cost of litigation. All facts plead therein are herein incorporated.

____

Subscribed and sworn to before me this __________ day of October, 1999.

____
Notary Public

PROOF OF SERVICE

The undersigned certifies that a copy of the foregoing instrument was served upon the attorneys of record of all parties to the above cause by enclosing the same in an envelope addressed to such attorneys at their business address as disclosed by the pleadings of record herein, with postage fully prepaid and by depositing said envelope in the U.S. Post Office mail box in Carbondale, Illinois, on the _____ day of ____________________, 2000.

____
Ronald Isaacs

STATE OF ILLINOIS
IN THE CIRCUIT COURT OF THE __JUDICIAL CIRCUIT
___________ COUNTY, ILLINOIS

CHRISTOPHER	)	
	)	
Plaintiff,	)	
	)	
v.	)	CASE
	)	
M S	)	
	)	
Defendant.	)	

PETITION TO DETERMINE PATERNITY

NOW COMES the Plaintiff, CHRISTOPHER by his attorney, Ronald L. Isaacs, and for his Petition to Determine Paternity states:

1. This action is brought pursuant to the provisions of the Illinois Parentage Act of 1984, §750 ILCS 45/1, et seq.

2. The MINOR CHILD is due to be born the first week of April, 1995.

3. The mother of the MINOR CHILD is M , who resides at 804 Street, , Illinois, 62271.

4. The presumed father of the child is CHRISTOPHER , who resides at South Moore, Illinois, 62263.

5. The parents of M ave stated they intend to deny CHRISTOPHER access to his child and assume guardianship of the child from their daughter without Plaintiff's consent or notice.

6. That it is in the best interest of the MINOR CHILD that a natural parent, the Plaintiff, have custody of the MINOR CHILD and **bond with the child immediately after birth** and that the Child's last name be recorded as ____________on the birth certificate..

WHEREFORE Plaintiff prays:

1. That the Court determine the existence of a father and child relationship.

2. That the natural father of the MINOR CHILD be ordered to do the following;

   a.) pay support to M during her pregnancy;
   b.) pay a sum certain for the support of the MINOR CHILD determined pursuant to the guidelines set forth in §750 ILCS 5/505; from the child's birth until custody is determined.
   c.) provide and/or maintain health/ hospitalization insurance coverage for the MINOR CHILD by adding the child to an existing insurance policy. Said insurance policy will cover the childs birth expenses;

3. That the natural father be allowed to bond with the MINOR CHILD **at birth or immediately there after and that the natural father be allowed to care for the child while the child is in the hospital nursery.**

4. That after the child goes home from the hospital the natural father be allowed maximum involvement and visitation pursuant to §750 ILCS 5/607 AND §750 ILCS 5/602© until custody is determined, including visits from Friday at 6pm until Sunday at 6 PM and from Tuesdays at 6pm until Wednesdays at 8 PM.

5. That Defendant claim her maternity expenses on her father's medical coverage which currently covers her medical expenses.

6. That reasonable child support be awarded Plaintiff if he is awarded custody.

7. That the child's last name be xxxxx.

8. That the Court grant any other and further relief that is deemed just.

____

CHRISTOPHER

____

RONALD L. ISAACS, Attorney

VERIFICATION

The undersigned, being first duly sworn on oath deposes and states that the contents of the foregoing document are true (except as to matter alleged to be on information and belief and those he believes to be true).

____

CHRISTOPHER

Subscribed and sworn to before me this __________ day of __________________, 2000.

____

Notary Public

STATE OF ILLINOIS)
) SS.
COUNTY OF JACKSON)

AFFIDAVIT

I, ________________________________, certify that I have read the foregoing document and that to the best of my knowledge, information, and belief formed after reasonable inquiry it is well grounded in fact and is warranted by existing law or a good faith argument for the extension, modification, or reversal of existing law and that it is not interposed for any improper purpose, such as to harass or to cause unnecessary delay or a needless increase in the cost of litigation. All facts plead therein are herein incorporated.

____

CRISTOPHER

Subscribed and sworn to before me this __________ day of __________________, 2000.

____

Notary Public

IN THE CIRCUIT COURT OF THE _____ JUDICIAL CIRCUIT
___________________ COUNTY, ILLINOIS

IN RE:THE MARRIAGE OF	)	
	)	
KELLY XXXXXXXXXX ,	)	
Petitioner,	)	
V.	)	**NO 93 D**
JAMES XXXXXXXXXX ,	)	
Respondent	)	

PETITION FOR RULE TO SHOW CAUSE

NOW COMES the Respondent, JAMES XXXXXXXXXXX, by and through his attorney, Ronald L. Isaacs, and, as his Petition for Rule to Show Cause, attaches his sworn affidavit and states:

1. On October 17, 1998 an Order was entered in case Number 93-D-XX, in the Circuit Court of XXXXXXX County, Illinois.

2. That Paragraph two (2) of said Order states:

"The Petitioner's income is approximately $1000.00 per month and that she shall pay $200.00 per month child support to respondent through the Circuit Clerk of Williamson County and that an Order of withholding shall be entered."

3. Petitioner Kelley XXXXX has willfully failed and refused to comply with the above quoted paragraph two (2) of the Order in that she has not paid any child support whatsoever to date.

4. On October 17, 1998 another Order was entered in the Circuit Court of XXXXXXXXX County, Illinois.

5. That paragraph one (1) of said Order states:

"Petitioner is in Contempt of Court."

6. That paragraph three (3) of said Order states:

"Petitioner Kelly XXXXXXXshall pay James XXXXXX $500.00 as reimbursement for attorney fees incurred."

7. Petitioner Kelley XXXXXXXXX has willfully failed and refused to comply with the above-quoted paragraph three (3) of the Order in that she has not paid any money as reimbursement for attorney fees incurred.

8. That Petitioner's conduct has been willful, contumacious, and in utter disregard of the subject Orders of this Honorable Court.

9. That Respondent has been compelled to retain legal counsel to pursue enforcement of said Orders and for the preparation and presentation of this Petition and is entitled to the payment of his reasonable attorneys' fees and costs by Petitioner.

10. That, pursuant to Section 505(c), each monthly payment constitutes a judgment in the amount of the monthly payment entered as of the date due, and each judgment bears interest of 9% per annum in accordance with Sections 735 ILCS 5/12-109 and 735 ILCS 5/2-1303 of the Illinois Code of Civil Procedure

.

WHEREFORE the Respondent, James XXXXXXXXXX, prays this Honorable Court as follows:

A. That this Honorable Court issue an Order or Rule to Show cause, if any she has, why she should not be held in contempt of this Honorable Court and punished accordingly for her wilful failure and refusal, without cause or justification to pay monthly child support as in the October 17, 1994 Order required or to pay the $500.00 reimbursement as the October 17, 1994 Order required.

B. That an Order issue requiring Petitioner Kelley XXXXXXXXXX instanter to pay to Respondent, James XXXXXXXXXXX, the support arrearage of $_________, plus accrued interest, or the sum as is then due and owing, and a judgment for this amount be entered in favor of respondent as against Petitioner.

C. That an Order issue requiring Petitioner Kelley xxxxxxxxxxxxx, instanter to pay to Respondent, James xxxxxxxxxxxxx, the amount of $500.00, plus accrued interest, or the sum then due and owing, and a judgment for this amount be entered in favor of the Respondent against Petitioner.

D. That an Order for withholding of Respondents income issue pursuant to Section 706.1 of the Illinois Marriage and Dissolution of Marriage Act, with this order to take effect instanter.

E. That Respondent, James xxxxxxxxxxxxxx, be granted his reasonable attorneys fees of $500.00 and costs pursuant to Section 508(b) of the Illinois Marriage and Dissolution of Marriage Act and a judgment for these fees and costs be entered in his favor as against Petitioner.

F. That Respondent, James XXXXXXXXXXXX, have all other and further relief as this Honorable Court deems just and equitable.

____

James XXXXXXXX, Respondent

VERIFICATION

The undersigned, being first duly sworn on oath deposes and states that the contents of the foregoing document are true (except as to matter alleged to be on information and belief and those he believes to be true).

____

____

Subscribed and sworn to before me this __________ day of __________________, 1999.

____

Notary Public

STATE OF ILLINOIS)
) SS.
COUNTY OF JACKSON)

AFFIDAVIT

I, ______________________________, certify that I have read the foregoing document and that to the best of my knowledge, information, and belief formed after reasonable inquiry it is well grounded in fact and is warranted by existing law or a good faith argument for the extension, modification, or reversal of existing law and that it is not interposed for any improper purpose, such as to harass or to cause unnecessary delay or a needless increase in the cost of litigation. All facts plead therein are herein incorporated. __________________

Subscribed and sworn to before me this __________ day of __________________, 2000.

____

Notary Public

MOTION FOR CONCILIATION

IN THE CIRCUIT COURT OF THE __JUDICIAL CIRCUIT
___________ COUNTY, ILLINOIS

IN RE THE MARRIAGE OF:

_______________________,	)	
Petitioner,	)	
v.	)	Case:
__________________________,	)	
Respondent.	)	

MOTION FOR CONCILIATION

NOW COMES the Respondent_____________________, by her attorney ______________, and respectfully moves the Court to order a conciliation conference and counseling, and in support thereof states as follows:

1. ______________________ of the Illinois Revised Statutes provides for a conciliation conference and counseling where there is a "prospect of reconciliation" of the marriage.

2. There is a prospect of reconciliation of the parties' marriage.

3. Proper skilled assistance through marriage counseling is available in the area of the parties residence, specifically ____________ and ___________ in _______________ Illinois.

4. _______________________ of the Illinois revised statutes mandates that the Illinois Marriage and Dissolution of Marriage Act

> "... shall be liberally construed and applied to promote its underlying purposes, which are to:
>
> (2) strengthen and preserve the integrity of marriage and safeguard family relationships..."

5. _____________ states as a second underlying purpose of the Act is to:

> "mitigate the potential harm to the spouses and their children caused by the process of legal dissolution."

6. The Respondent, and the parties children are being harmed by the process of the parties' legal dissolution.

7. Marriage counseling would mitigate the harm to the parties' children and the spouses.

8. Respondent is willing to pay the costs of counseling.

WHEREFORE Respondent respectfully prays this Court to enter an order for conciliation and counseling and for such other relief as may be deemed equitable and just.

(Insert signatures and proof of service here)

Appendix

NOTE: Other forms that are useful for litigation of these issues and actually proven successful in court are in the *Divorce/Custody Kit and Guide to Fathers' Rights* by the author. A table of contents may be seen at http://www. fathers-rights. com .

The documents are also available on CD at http://www.courttips.com The *Guide to Fathers' Rights* also contains tactics and a sample cross-examination successfully used to win custody cases.

APP. 1A

(insert case heading and number here)

MOTION TO DISMISS ORDER OF PROTECTION AND FOR SANCTIONS

Comes now the FIELD(Petitioner or Respondent) by FIELD(His or Her) attorney FIELD(Our Attorney) and for his motion states:

1. That case FIELD(CASE NUMBER) is pending in *(insert county)* concerning the alleged abuse of KEYBOARD(Name of abused).

2. That in an immediate response to FIELD(Petitioner or Respondent)'s petition for FIELD(Is Spouse petitioner or Respondent)'s mental records filed in that case, Plaintiff filed for a protective order in KEYBOARD(Venue?).

3. That FIELD(Is Spouse petitioner or Respondent)'s allegations of abuse by FIELD(Petitioner or Respondent) and FIELD(Spouse Pronoun His or Her) residency in the petition for protective order are contrary to FIELD(Spouse Pronoun His or Her) sworn testimony in the above case and FIELD(Is Spouse petitioner or Respondent) attempts to avoid being held to her sworn testimony by forum shopping.

4. That FIELD(Is Spouse petitioner or Respondent) falsely alleges residency in KEYBOARD(County?) to prevent FIELD(Petitioner or Respondent) from visiting the child of the parties.

5. That said pleading is false and made solely to harass and intimidate FIELD(Petitioner or Respondent) into forgoing FIELD(His or Her) efforts to seek FIELD(Is Spouse petitioner or Respondent)'s mental records and exercise FIELD(His or Her) visitation with the parties' child.

6. That FIELD(Petitioner or Respondent) has incurred reasonable attorney fees responding to the false pleading which should be paid by FIELD(Is Spouse petitioner or Respondent) under Supreme Court rule 137.

Wherefore FIELD(Petitioner or Respondent) moves this Court to dismiss FIELD(CASE NUMBER), for reasonable attorney fees incurred to respond to the Protective Order and for such other relief the court deems just.

____

Our Attorney,
Attorney for FIELD(Petitioner or Respondent)

PROOF OF SERVICE

The undersigned certifies that a copy of the foregoing instrument was served upon:

FIELD(FULL NAME OF OPPOSING ATTORNEY)
FIELD(6 Street Address)
FIELD(6 Suite or P.O.)
FIELD(6 City State Zip)

by enclosing the same in an envelope addressed as shown above, with postage fully prepaid, and by depositing said envelope in a U.S. Post Office mailbox in *(insert name of place),* on the _____ day of ______________________, 20_____.

____

FIELD(Our Attorney)

FIELD(FIRM NAME)
ATTORNEY AT LAW
(address of attorney)
(telephone)

APP. 1B
MOTION TO DISMISS/VACATE ORDER OF PROTECTION AND TO CONSOLIDATE CASES

COMES NOW, the Respondent/husband, BRIAN , by and through His undersigned attorneys, and files this His motion , in the above entitled cause and in support thereof respectfully states as follows:

1. Respondent has a meritorious defense to the order of protection,

2. Petitioner knew how to contact Respondent yet failed to do so and obtained a protective order exparte based on false and dated claims .

3. The most current act complained of was October 1995 (before the parties' divorce) and attached threatening notes from 1991, indicating there was no basis for an emergency exparte order with no notice to Petitioner.

4. That since obtaining the ex-parte order, Petitioner filed a false police report (proven "unfounded" by police officers) in an attempt to harass Respondent into forgoing visitation with his children by having him arrested. **Denying the children visitation with their father is a form of mental child abuse not in the children's best interests**.

5. That Petitioner has been confined for mental problems and is exhibiting a pattern of actions she used on previous spouses to remove them from their children's lives.(or she should be examined for possible mental problems)

6. That Respondent Brian is petitioning to vacate or modify his Judgement of Dissolution dated October 2, 1997 in 97 D 210 because it was obtained by fraud and misrepresentation as evidenced by Petitioner filing for a protective order on October 3,1997 and filing false police reports in an attempt to prevent visitation immediately after obtaining the Judgement despite contrary language in the settlement agreement. **Respondent now seeks sole custody**.

7. That the Protective order should be dismissed and sanctions and fees awarded under Rule 137 against Petitioner and **ANY PARTY AUTHORIZED BY LAW TO ASSIST IN DRAFTING PETITIONS FOR ORDERS OF PROTECTION** that assisted Petitioner in drafting her Petition and that this protective order case (97OP4)should be consolidated with family law case 97D2 for consideration of all inter related issues with a common core of fact.

WHEREFORE, the RESPONDENT, BRIAN , moves this Court to vacate the order of protection, for consolidation of cases ,for attorney fees and sanctions and for such other relief the court deems just .

____
Respondent

APP. 2A

(insert case heading here)

Petition for Mental Examination

Now comes the Petitioner and for his petition states:

1. The mental health of a potential custodian is a factor for consideration in custody awards under 750 ILCS 5/602(5), Best Interests of Child.

2. Respondent has been engaging in Satanism and Occultism and has manifested aberrant behavior including two attempted suicides, irrational behavior, excessive gambling, placing lit cigarettes near Petitioner's face, apparent self infliction of a burn **and filing of a false petition for an order of protection**.

3. Said behaviors, if not diagnosed and treated, could lead to endangerment of the children of the parties.

4. The health insurance of the parties will cover the cost of the mental examination, testing and treatment.

Wherefore Petitioner prays the court order a mental examination of the Respondent and for such other relief the court deems necessary.

(signatures here)
(insert proof of service here)

APP. 2B

Motion for Mental Competence Examination

COMES NOW, the Respondent/Husband, JOSEPH A. DOE, by and through His undersigned attorneys, and files this His motion , in the above entitled cause and in support thereof respectfully states as follows:

1. Petitioner has exhibited a pattern of emotional instability resulting in her throughout the years since the divorce of the parties filing repeated false allegations of misconduct of the Respondent in an effort to deprive him of his rights to contact, maximum involvement with and have a meaningful relationship with his children.

2. Petitioner has never proven any of her spurious allegations.

3. Said allegations impact adversely on and seriously endanger the mental and emotional health of the children.

4. Petitioner is in need of emotional counseling and psychological evaluation

WHEREFORE, the Respondent/Husband, JOSEPH A.DOE, moves this Court for a mental /psychological evaluation of the Petitioner and that the results be made available only to the Court for aid in determining custody/ visitation issues in this case.

Attorney for Husband, _______________________________
(insert name)

PROOF OF SERVICE

The undersigned certifies that a copy of the foregoing instruments was served upon :

MICHAEL
123 South County
Suite H1
JACKSON IL 60187

by enclosing the same in an envelope addressed to the address as disclosed by the pleadings of record herein, with postage fully prepaid, and by depositing said envelope in the U.S. Post Office mail box in Carbondale, Illinois, on the __day of _______, 20__.

____

IN THE CIRCUIT COURT OF THE EIGHTEENTH JUDICIAL CIRCUIT
FROMAGE COUNTY, ILLINOIS

In Re: The Marriage of:	)	
	)	
JOANNE E. DOE	)	
Petitioner,	)	
and	)	CASE NO.: 96 D 007
	)	
JOSEPH A. DOE	)	
	)	
Respondent	)	

ORDER

THIS CAUSE having come on to be heard on the Respondent/Husband, JOSEPH A. DOE'S motion, and the Court having reviewed the pleadings and heard testimony and being duly advised in the premises **FINDS** that the Motion should be and is hereby **GRANTED.**

____
J U D G E   DATE

IN THE CIRCUIT COURT OF THE EIGHTEENTH JUDICIAL CIRCUIT
FROMAGE COUNTY, ILLINOIS

In Re: The Marriage of:	)	
	)	
JOANNE E. DOE	)	
	)	
Petitioner,	)	
and	)	CASE NO.: 96 D 007
	)	
JOSEPH A. DOE	)	
	)	
Respondent.	)	

NOTICE OF HEARING

To: MICHAEL, Esquire
310 South County
Suite H 1
JACKSON IL 60187

PLEASE TAKE NOTICE that on the __ day of December, 2006, at __a.m., or as soon thereafter as counsel can be heard, the undersigned will bring on to be heard Respondent/Husband, before the Honorable R. HANGEM, Circuit Judge, in the Fromage County Courthouse, , Illinois.

____
Ronald L. Isaacs
Attorney at Law

APP. 2C

BRIEF IN SUPPORT OF MOTION TO COMPEL MENTAL EXAMINATION AND PRODUCTION OF MENTAL RECORDS TO THE COURT ONLY

NOW COMES the Respondent, TIMOTHY JONES, by and through his attorney, Ronald L. Isaacs, and for his brief states as follows:

1. That the mental health of the parties is a factor for the Court to consider to determine the best interests of the child under 750 ILCS 5/602(5) and a mental examination of the Petitioner by a Court Appointed examiner and production of the result of said exam and all of Petitioners records of previous mental treatments to the court alone would enable the Court to properly evaluate the mental condition of the Petitioner. The Respondent **DOES NOT** request that confidential mental treatment information be made available to him, but **ONLY** to the Court.

2. The Court has an **absolute right to compel a mental examination** of the Plaintiff, especially when she refuses to voluntarily release records of her previous mental records to the court by claiming the confidentiality privilege under 740 ILCS 110/10. This was made clear in a first district case **upholding** the confidentiality privilege as follows: "We are mindful of the welfare of the children and note that psychiatric testimony deemed necessary to determine the best interests of the children may be obtained via the court ordered psychiatric examination." **In re marriage of Kimberly Ann Lombaer and Forest Lumbar. Jr.** 200 Ill.App.3d 712 ; 558 N.E. 2d 388 Appellate Court of Illinois, First District, Third Division June 27, 1990.

3. The First district has consistently upheld the confidentiality privilege when the patient has not raised the issue of her mental treatment including as recently as 1998 in **Mandiara v Canulli**, 299 Ill. App. 3rd 593; 701 N.E. 2d 127 but the Federal Court, Northern District, Eastern Division, interpreting the Illinois law on confidentiality of mental records in 1983 stated:

"In any event , the act permits disclosure of communications where the patient's mental condition is an element of a claim or defenseafter an in camera inspection of the court. Id 810(a)(1)-(2). That is exactly what happened here. Plaintiff's fitness as a mother was certainly at issue in the custody proceedings...," **Bond V. Pecaut**, 561 F. Supp. 1037; 1983 U.S. Dist. Lexis 17793

4. That the Respondent has stated in his sworn motion a well grounded belief that Petitioner has mental problems in that he believes Petitioner is taking anti-depressant medications, has contemplated suicide and/or hurting herself, has punished the child of the parties by slapping him in the face, hitting him with a wooden spoon, and forcing him into cold showers and that Petitioner has engaged in several explosive emotional outbursts in front of witnesses.

5. Respondent fears that Petitioner will not testify truthfully about her mental condition and that without an in-camera review of her prior mental records and/or a new psychological evaluation by a court appointed psychologist, the Court will have no basis to determine the credibility of the Petitioner's testimony. In Illinois criminal cases the privilege of confidentiality has been ignored when credibility is at issue: "In spite of the statutory privilege, it is well established that the mental history of a witness is relevant to his credibility and a permissible area of impeachment." People v. Lindsey(1979),73 Ill.App 3d 436, 392 N.E. 2nd 278 "...Almost any emotional or mental defect may materially affect the accuracy of the testimony. A conservative list of such defects would have to include a psychosis, most neuroses, defects in the structure of the nervous system, mental deficience, alcoholism, drug addiction, and psychopathic personality ..." **People of the State of Illinois v. Clarence Dace 114 Ill App. 3d 908; 449 N.E. 2d 1031 (Third District, 1983)**

6. That a fair and just custody hearing cannot be held without **all** factors of 750 ILCS 5/602 being considered including subparagraph (5), "the mental and physical health of all individuals involved."

"Since there was no fair or adequate consideration of **all** the aforementioned (best interest) factors, we reverse the order granting forest temporary custody." **In re marriage of Kimberly Ann Lombaer and Forest Lumbar. Jr.** 200 Ill.App.3d 712 ; 558 N.E. 2d 388 Appellate Court of Illinois, First District, Third Division June 27, 1990.

7. Respondent does not request an examination of the mental health records, only that the court examine the records in-camera but does request that names of treating psychiatrists /doctors be provided to Respondent so that Respondent can ensure the court is receiving any voluntarily provided records. The names of treating doctors are not privileged information. "It is evident that disclosure of the patient's name does not violate the physician-patient privilege...As Geisenberger pointed out, the name of the patient generally has no relation to the ailment of treatment and is therefore not privileged information." **House V. Swedish American Hospital**, 206 Ill. App. 3d 437; 564 N.E. 2d 922

In summary, if the Petitioner insists on exercising her confidentiality privilege and the court rules that she does have such a privilege, an examination of Petitioner by a Court appointed psychologist will be required to adequately address **all** elements of the best interest standard for a custody modification judgment. The examiner should be advised of the allegations contained in Respondent's motion for an examination. Petitioner should bear the expense of such an examination or in the alternative provide full disclosure of her mental/depression treatments and medications to the court for an in- camera review.

Respectfully submitted,

____

APP. 3

MOTION FOR DEFENDANT DISCOVERY

NOW COMES Defendant,-----, by counsel, Ronald L. Isaacs, and moves that the People of the State of Illinois be ordered to make the following disclosures to Defendant.

A.

1. Furnish the identity and location of witnesses who will testify at trial together with the subject matter of their testimony, including:

(a) their relevant written or recorded statements;

(b) memoranda containing substantially verbatim reports of their oral statements;

(c) a list of memoranda which report or summarize any statements made by them;

(d) the transcript of any testimony given by them before the grand jury, and;

(e) any record of prior criminal convictions suffered by any of them which may be used for the purpose of impeachment.

2. The names and last known addresses of all persons having knowledge of any facts relevant to the charges made against Defendant irrespective of whether the State intends to call such witnesses at the trial, together with;

(a) their written or recorded statements:

(b) memoranda containing substantially verbatim reports of their oral statements;

(c) a list of memoranda which report or summarize any statements made by them, and;

(d) the transcript of any testimony given by them before the grand jury which returned the indictment herein.

B.

3. All material and information within the knowledge, possession or control of the State which tends to negate the guilt of the Defendant, or reduce the offense with which he is charged to a lesser offense, or reduce his punishment for any offense of which he is convicted in these proceedings.

C.

4. Any written or recorded statements and the substance of any oral statements made by Defendant and the names and last known addresses of all persons who witnessed the making or acknowledgment of such statements.

D.

5. Any books , papers, documents, photographs or tangible objects which are in any way related to or were obtained as a result of the investigation of the charge made against the Defendant and which are in the knowledge, possession, or control of the State, irrespective of whether the State intends to use such items in any trial or hearing held herein.

6. Any statements (or reports summarizing such statements) obtained from any person during the course of the investigation of the charges made against the Defendant which are in the possession, control, or knowledge of the State.

7. Any reports, memoranda or writing of any kind or character relating to the charges made against the Defendant which are in the possession or control or knowledge of the State, excluding there from the trial plans or strategy of the State's Attorney.

8. Disclosure as to whether or not the Defendant was viewed by the complaining witness or any other potential witness for identification purposes, and, if so, with regard thereto:

(a) the time, date, and place of such viewing:

(b) the names and last known addresses of the persons present at such viewing:

(c) whether or not the Defendant was identified at such viewing, and;

(d) the names and last known addresses of the persons making such identification.

9. Disclosure as to whether there has been as electronic surveillance by any governmental agency or person of any conversation to which Defendant's counsel was a party.

E.

10. Any reports or statements of tests or analysis made by experts in connection with the items referred to in paragraph five above.

FURTHER, the Defendant requests that the Court make its order a continuing order upon the State to the extent that the State be required to disclose such material as indicated above which may come into the possession of, or become known to, the State in the future.

Respectfully submitted,

____

PROOF OF SERVICE

THE UNDERSIGNED certifies that a copy of the foregoing MOTION FOR DEFENDANT DISCOVERY was served upon the attorneys of record of all parties to the above cause by enclosing the same in an envelope addressed to such attorneys at the business addresses as disclosed by the pleadings of record and with postage fully prepaid and then by depositing the same in a United States Post Office Mailbox in______, Illinois, on this _____ day of______________,2002

____

Ronald L. Isaacs

APP. 4

(insert case heading and number here)

MOTION TO CONTINUE

NOW COMES the Defendant, Ronnie DOE by and through his attorney, RONALD L. ISAACS, and moves the Court for a continuance, and in support of said Motion respectfully states as follows:

1. The above entitled case has been set for jury docket on May 12, 1997 at 9:00 a.m.

2. Defendant's attorney has just entered his appearance and **no discovery has been completed.**

3. That Attorney Isaacs has conflicts on the following dates in July: 3rd, 7th, 8th, 17th, 18th.

WHEREFORE the Defendant prays the Court continue this cause to the MONTH OF JULY or AUGUST, and for such further relief the Court deems equitable and just.

(Insert PROOF OF SERVICE here)

Signatures as in APP. 1

<u>VERIFIED PETITION FOR RULE TO SHOW CAUSE</u>

COMES NOW the RESPONDENT, Aaron DODDS by and through his undersigned attorney and files this his Petition for Rule to Show Cause, and in support thereof respectfully states as follows:

1. That on JANUARY 4, 2000, this Court **(JUDGE FLoyd)** entered an order setting visitation in the above entitled case.

2. That paragraph 1a sets visitation for respondent to"The second full weekend of each and every month from 12 midnight until Sunday at 3 pm.

3. Petitioner, LeAnn DODDS has willfully failed and refused to comply with the above quoted paragraphs of the Order in that she denied visitation on the second weekends in February and March when she **filed a false and malicious abuse report** against Respondent's stepchild with DCFS(found unfounded) ,did not request a visitation plan from DCFS ,and willfully refused to obey the Court's ordered visitation schedule.

4. That Petitioner, LeAnnDODDS **has previously been required by Judge Floyd to pay Respondent's attorney fees for violating visitation provisions** of this Court's order and exhibits a **pattern of refusals** to follow the court's orders and of making unfounded allegations of abuse in order to deny court ordered visitation to Respondent.

5. That Petitioner's conduct has been willful, contumacious, and in utter disregard of the subject Orders of this Honorable Court and emotionally damaging to the children of the parties.

6. That Petitioner has been compelled to retain legal counsel to pursue enforcement of said Orders and for the preparation and presentation of this Petition and **is entitled to the payment of his reasonable attorneys' fees and costs by Petitioner**, LeAnn DODDS.

7. **It is requested that hearing on this Petition** be held concurrently with hearings on Respondent's Petition to modify custody.

WHEREFORE, the Respondent respectfully prays this Court enter a Rule to Show Cause and for reasonable attorney fees and expenses to be paid by Petitioner to Respondent and for such other relief the court deems necessary and just.

For the Respondent

VERIFICATION and AFFFIDAVIT

Under penalties as provided by law pursuant to Section 1-109 of the Code of Civil Procedure, the undersigned certifies that the statements set forth in this instrument are true and correct, except as to matters therein stated to be on information and belief and as to such matters the undersigned certifies as aforesaid that he believes the same to be. All statements made above are herein incorporated as if they were specifically typed within this affidavit.

DATED:______________________

____

Aaron DODDS

Signed by Aaron DODDS and sworn before me this __ day of ___ 2002.

State of Illinois

County of _______

____

NOTARY PUBLIC, my commission expires _____

PROOF OF SERVICE

The undersigned certifies that a copy of the foregoing instrument was served upon:

Richard WHITE
P.O. Box 37
Chancey, IL. 62231

by enclosing the same in an envelope addressed as shown above, with postage fully prepaid, and by depositing said envelope in a U.S. Post Office mailbox in *(insert name of place)*, on the (*th) day of (*month*), 2002.

____

Ronald L. Isaacs
10325 Winterhue Dr.
Baton Rouge, LA. 70810
225 757 0607

(CASE HEADING HERE)

RULE TO SHOW CAUSE

IT IS HEREBY ORDERED THAT a Rule to Show Cause is entered against Petitioner, LeAnn DODDS commanding her to appear before this Court on the _______ day of __________, 2002, at the hour of ____________ o'clock, to show good cause, if any, why she should not be held in contempt of this Court for failing to allow visitation as previously ordered by this Court and why she should not reimburse Respondent for legal fees of $700.00 incurred to enforce the Courts order

Entered this ___ day of _______, 2002.

____

JUDGE

APP. 5

(Insert case heading and number here)

ENTRY OF APPEARANCE, PLEA AND JURY DEMAND

NOW COMES **RONALD L. ISAACS**, Attorney at Law ,(or John Doe Pro Se) and

1. Enters his appearance (on behalf of the Defendant John Doe,)(or PRO SE) and requests that all copies of pleadings, documents and correspondence be forwarded to him at his office address as disclosed herein,

2. Enters a plea of **NOT GUILTY** to the charges in the above entitled cases, and

3. Demands **Jury Trial** .

____

John Doe. pro Se

(insert PROOF OF SERVICE here)

John Doe
Street
City, State, Zip
Telephone

APP.6
Typical Domestic Violence Statute

NOTE PARAGRAPH V - VISITATION DENIAL IS DOMESTIC VIOLENCE!

§ 750 ILCS 60/103. Definitions

Sec. 103. Definitions. For the purposes of this Act, the following terms shall have the following meanings:
(1) "Abuse" means physical abuse, harassment, intimidation of a dependent, interference with personal liberty or willful deprivation but does not include reasonable direction of a minor child by a parent or person in loco parentis.
(2) "Adult with disabilities" means an elder adult with disabilities or a high-risk adult with disabilities. A person may be an adult with disabilities for purposes of this Act even though he or she has never been adjudicated an incompetent adult. However, no court proceeding may be initiated or continued on behalf of an adult with disabilities over that adult's objection, unless such proceeding is approved by his or her legal guardian, if any.
(3) "Domestic violence" means abuse as defined in paragraph (1).
(4) "Elder adult with disabilities" means an adult prevented by advanced age from taking appropriate action to protect himself or herself from abuse by a family or household member.
(5) "Exploitation" means the illegal, including tortious, use of a high-risk adult with disabilities or of the assets or resources of a high-risk adult with disabilities. Exploitation includes, but is not limited to, the misappropriation of assets or resources of a high-risk adult with disabilities by undue influence, by breach of a fiduciary relationship, by fraud, deception, or extortion, or the use of such assets or resources in a manner contrary to law.
(6) "Family or household members" include spouses, former spouses, parents, children, stepchildren and other persons related by blood or by present or prior marriage, persons who share or formerly shared a common dwelling, persons who have or allegedly have a child in common, persons who share or allegedly share a blood relationship through a child, persons who have or have had a dating or engagement relationship, and persons with disabilities and their personal assistants. For purposes of this paragraph, neither a casual acquaintanceship nor ordinary fraternization between 2 individuals in business or social contexts shall be deemed to constitute a dating relationship. In the case of a high-risk adult with disabilities, "family or household members" includes any person who has the responsibility for a high-risk adult as a result of a family relationship or who has assumed responsibility for all or a portion of the care of a high-risk adult with disabilities voluntarily, or by express or implied contract, or by court order.
(7) **"Harassment"** means knowing conduct which is not necessary to accomplish a purpose that is reasonable under the circumstances; would cause a reasonable person emotional distress; and does cause emotional distress to the petitioner. Unless the presumption is rebutted by a preponderance of the evidence, the following types of conduct shall be presumed to cause emotional distress:
(i) creating a disturbance at petitioner's place of employment or school;
(ii) repeatedly telephoning petitioner's place of employment, home or residence;
(iii) repeatedly following petitioner about in a public place or places;

(iv) repeatedly keeping petitioner under surveillance by remaining present outside his or her home, school, place of employment, vehicle or other place occupied by petitioner or by peering in petitioner's windows;

(v) **improperly concealing a minor child from petitioner, repeatedly threatening to improperly remove a minor child of petitioner's from the jurisdiction or from the physical care of petitioner, repeatedly threatening to conceal a minor child from petitioner, or making a single such threat following an actual or attempted improper removal or concealment**, unless respondent was fleeing an incident or pattern of domestic violence; or

(vi) threatening physical force, confinement or restraint on one or more occasions.

(8) "High-risk adult with disabilities" means a person aged 18 or over whose physical or mental disability impairs his or her ability to seek or obtain protection from abuse, neglect, or exploitation.

(9) "Interference with personal liberty" means committing or threatening physical abuse, harassment, intimidation or willful deprivation so as to compel another to engage in conduct from which she or he has a right to abstain or to refrain from conduct in which she or he has a right to engage.

(10) "Intimidation of a dependent" means subjecting a person who is dependent because of age, health or disability to participation in or the witnessing of: physical force against another or physical confinement or restraint of another which constitutes physical abuse as defined in this Act, regardless of whether the abused person is a family or household member.

(11) (A) "Neglect" means the failure to exercise that degree of care toward a high-risk adult with disabilities which a reasonable person would exercise under the circumstances and includes but is not limited to:

(i) the failure to take reasonable steps to protect a high-risk adult with disabilities from acts of abuse;

(ii) the repeated, careless imposition of unreasonable confinement;

(iii) the failure to provide food, shelter, clothing, and personal hygiene to a high-risk adult with disabilities who requires such assistance;

(iv) the failure to provide medical and rehabilitative care for the physical and mental health needs of a high-risk adult with disabilities; or

(v) the failure to protect a high-risk adult with disabilities from health and safety hazards.

(B) Nothing in this subsection (10) shall be construed to impose a requirement that assistance be provided to a high-risk adult with disabilities over his or her objection in the absence of a court order, nor to create any new affirmative duty to provide support to a high-risk adult with disabilities.

(12) "Order of protection" means an emergency order, interim order or plenary order, granted pursuant to this Act, which includes any or all of the remedies authorized by Section 214 of this Act [750 ILCS 60/214].

(13) "Petitioner" may mean not only any named petitioner for the order of protection and any named victim of abuse on whose behalf the petition is brought, but also any other person protected by this Act.

(14) "Physical abuse" includes sexual abuse and means any of the following:

(i) knowing or reckless use of physical force, confinement or restraint;

(ii) knowing, repeated and unnecessary sleep deprivation; or

(iii) knowing or reckless conduct which creates an immediate risk of physical harm.

(15) "Willful deprivation" means willfully denying a person who because of age, health or disability requires medication, medical care, shelter, accessible shelter or services, food, therapeutic device, or other physical assistance, and thereby exposing that person to the risk of physical, mental or emotional

harm, except with regard to medical care or treatment when the dependent person has expressed an intent to forgo such medical care or treatment. This paragraph does not create any new affirmative duty to provide support to dependent persons.
History
(Source: P.A. 86-542; 87-1186, § 3.)

Cross Reference:
For the contents of an order of protection, see 750 ILCS 60/221.

TRICK OF THE TRADE:

Use the threats of child concealment provision under "harassment" to get an order of protection against her BEFORE she gets one against you

STATE OF ILLINOIS
IN THE CIRCUIT COURT OF THE THIRD JUDICIAL CIRCUIT
MADISON COUNTY, ILLINOIS

JANE DOE, k/n/a **ROBIN JANE DOE** Plaintiff,	)))	
	)	
vs.	)	Case No. **87-D-000**
	)	
JOE DOE, Defendant.	))	

PETITION TO MODIFY CUSTODY ORDER

NOW COMES the Defendant, JOE DOE, by and through his attorney, RONALD L. ISAACS, and pursuant to 750 ILCS 5/610(b) prays the court to modify a custody Order, and in support of his Petition states as follows:

1. That on June 26, 1987 an order was entered in the above entitled cause that stated:

> "Permanent care, custody and control of the minor child is granted to JANE DOE".

2. That there are two minor children of the parties; namely Erica born October 21, 1986 and Jossica, born August 30, 1987.

3. That Pursuant to 750 ILCS 6/610(b) there has been a substantial change of circumstances of the parties and modification is in the best interest of the children as defined by 750 ILCS 6/602.

4. That said such substantial change of circumstances include:

A. That Plaintiff Robin JANE DOE has engaged in a comprehensive scheme to deny the children any type of relationship with their father.

B. That the children have made **false allegations of physical abuse by the father**.

C. That Defendant believes that the mother coached the children to make the false allegations of abuse.

D. That said false allegations are in retaliation for a letter written to Robin JANE DOE on July 13, 1995 detailing denials of visitation and requesting makeup visitation.

E. That the children may be suffering from **Parental Alienation Syndrome.**

> "A disturbance in which children are preoccupied with depreciation and criticism of a parent-denigration that is unjustified and/or exaggerated" Plumb, Gordon B., Ph.D., **Humanizing Custody Disputes**, Springfield Illinois, Thomas, 1990. Quoting Gardner, Richard A., **Child Custody Litigation**, New Jersey, Creative Therapeutics, 1986.
>
> "Parent Alienation syndrome is caused by the conscious or unconscious acts of one parent brainwashing or programming a child against the other parent" pp.71., Plumb.
>
> "Brainwashing has many obvious and extremely subtle variations. One parent may call the other names such as ...pervert." Plumb, pp. 72.
>
> "In more than half the cases in which we have been involved where PAS was a significant factor, sex-abuse allegations have also been made." Plumb, 74.

F. That there has been a continual pattern of visitation abuse, including late visitation and denial of visitation.

G. That since remarrying Robin JANE DOE has encouraged the children to use HER LAST name instead of THE FATHER'S LAST NAME without any Court order changing the childrens' names.

H. That the childrens' mental well being may be improved by a change of custody.

5. That pursuant to 750 ILCS 6/602 it is in the best interests of the minor children that permanent care, custody, and control of the minor children be awarded to the Father, JOE DOE.

6. That the father JOE DOE will foster the love and respect of the children towards both parents.

7. That the father JOE DOE will encourage and facilitate the relationship of the children towards **both** parents.

8. Robin JANE DOE is able to contribute to the support of the minor children.

WHEREFORE JOE DOE prays this court:

1. Award custody of the minor children to the father, JOE DOE,
2. Order Plaintiff Robin JANE DOE to pay reasonable child support, and
3. For such other relief the Court deems just and equitable.

MOTION FOR DEPOSITION OF CHILDREN OR IMMEDIATE IN-CHAMBERS EXAMINATION BY THE COURT AND VIDEO TAPING OF ALL INTERVIEWS OF THE CHILDREN.

COMES NOW, the Respondent, JOSEPH A. DOE by and through His undersigned attorney, files this motion in the above entitled cause and in support thereof respectfully states as follows:

1. Petitioner has exhibited a pattern of emotional instability resulting in her throughout the years since the divorce of the parties filing repeated false allegations of misconduct of the Respondent in an effort to deprive him of his rights to contact, maximum involvement with and have a meaningful relationship with his children.

2. Petitioner has never proven any of her spurious allegations.

3. Said allegations impact adversely on and seriously endanger the mental health and the emotional health of the children of the parties and constitute mental and emotional child abuse.

4. Petitioner has now evidently brainwashed the minor children into making **ever escalating** accusations of abuse to the point of possibly causing criminal actions to be filed against the Respondent.

5. It is imperative that a deposition of the children be taken to "pin down" the allegations of abuse before further accusations are suggested to the children intentionally by the Petitioner or unintentionally through incompetence of questioners.

6. That Petitioner refuses to allow a deposition of the children **despite reportedly having allowed the children to be interviewed at length by Petitioner's counsel without Respondent's counsel or a child's representative being present.**

7. That copies of all allegations of abuse by any party and tapes or notes of any interview regarding abuse of the children of the parties should be made available immediately to Respondent's counsel to ensure a fair hearing for Respondent.

8. That Dr. DOOLITTLE has reportedly offered copies of a taped interview of the children to third parties without consent of the court.

9. That producing the above records and tapes and allowing a deposition or in camera interview of the children are necessary for a fair custody evaluation or for setting any visitation schedule.

10. That video taping of all interviews of the children will expose any incompetence or leading questions that might tend to distort or falsify the future testimony of the children and should be ordered for all children's interviews by any party.

WHEREFORE, the Respondent/Husband, JOSEPH A. DOE moves this Court for **permission to immediately depose** the children of the parties **or in the alternative** that the Court conduct an **immediate in-camera interview** with the children for the purpose of pinning down all allegations of abuse and **eliminating the continued growth of false allegations** against the Petitioner and that the Court order any party having written notes or records or tapes of allegations of abuse to provide same immediately to Respondent's counsel and for such other relief the Court deems necessary.

____

Attorney for

APP. 9

A PARENT'S FUNDAMENTAL RIGHTS

(Illinois Supreme Court Quotes U.S. Supreme Court)

LULAY V LULAY

193 Ill. 2d 455 739 N.E. 2d 521 250 Ill. Dec 758 (Oct 26, 2000)

Fundamental Right

The fourteenth amendment [***23] to the United States Constitution provides that no state shall "deprive any person of life, liberty, or property, without due process of law." The due process clause "includes a substantive component that 'provides heightened protection against government interference with certain fundamental rights and liberty interests.' " Troxel, 530 U.S. at , 147 L. Ed. 2d at 56, 120 S. Ct. at 2059-60, quoting Washington v. [**530] Glucksberg, 521 U.S. 702, 720, 138 L. Ed. 2d 772, 787, 117 S. Ct. 2258, 2267 (1997).

As the United States Supreme Court stated in Troxel, the "liberty interest at issue in this case-the interest of parents in the care, custody, and control of their children-is perhaps the oldest of the fundamental liberty [*471] interests recognized by this Court." Troxel, 530 U.S. at , 147 L. Ed. 2d at 56, 120 S. Ct. at 2060 (reviewing Court decisions that have recognized and explained the fundamental interest of parents in the upbringing of their children); accord People v. R.G., 131 Ill. 2d 328, 342-43, 137 Ill. Dec. 588, 546 N.E.2d 533 (1989) (upholding the constitutionality of the "Minors Requiring Authoritative Intervention" [***24] statutes (see Ill. Rev. Stat. 1987, ch. 37, par. 803-1 et seq.) and recognizing that, under United States Supreme Court precedent, "parents have a liberty interest in bearing and raising their children").

In Meyer v. Nebraska, 262 U.S. 390, 67 L. Ed. 1042, 43 S. Ct. 625 (1923), the Court held unconstitutional a statute that prohibited the teaching of certain foreign languages at an elementary school. The Court reasoned that the due process clause protects the rights of parents to "establish a home and bring up children" and "to control the education of their own." Meyer, 262 U.S. at 399, 401, 67 L. Ed. at 1045, 1046, 43 S. Ct. at 626, 627. Two years later, in Pierce v. Society of the Sisters of the Holy Names of Jesus & Mary, 268 U.S. 510, 69 L. Ed. 1070, 45 S. Ct. 571 (1925), the Court held unconstitutional a statute that required parents to send their children to public schools, reasoning that the statute interfered with the liberty right of parents "to direct the upbringing and education of children under their control." The Pierce Court explained that the "child is not the mere creature of the State; those who nurture [***25] him and direct his destiny have the right, coupled with the high duty, to recognize and prepare him for additional obligations." Pierce, 268 U.S. at 535, 69 L. Ed. at 1078, 45 S. Ct. at 573.

Years later, the fundamental right of parents to raise their children remained an important focus in the jurisprudence of the United State Supreme Court. In Stanley v. Illinois, 405 U.S. 645, 31 L. Ed. 2d 551, 92 S. Ct. 1208 [*472] (1972), the Court held unconstitutional a statute that declared that, upon the death of the mother, children of unwed fathers became wards of the state. The Court reasoned: "The private interest here, that of a man in the children he has sired and raised, undeniably warrants deference and, absent a powerful countervailing interest, protection. It is plain that the interest of a parent in the companionship, care, custody, and management of his or her children 'comes to this Court with a momentum for respect lacking when appeal is made to liberties which derive merely from shifting economic arrangements.' [Citation.]" Stanley, 405 U.S. at 651, 31 L. Ed. 2d at 558, 92 S. Ct. at 1212.

Soon after, in Wisconsin v. Yoder, 406 U.S. 205, 32 L. Ed. 2d 15, 92 S. Ct. 1526 (1972), [***26] the Court held, albeit primarily on the basis of the first amendment right to free exercise of religion, that a state's compulsory education law did not apply to a group of Amish children. The Court emphasized: "The history and culture of Western civilization reflect a strong tradition of parental concern for the nurture and upbringing of their children. This primary role of the parents in the upbringing of their children is now established beyond debate as an enduring American tradition." Yoder, 406 U.S. at 232, 32 L. Ed. 2d at 35, 92 S. Ct. at 1541-42; see also Santosky v. Kramer, 455 U.S. 745, 753, 71 L. Ed. 2d 599, 606, 102 S. Ct. 1388, 1394 (1982) (determining the standard of proof necessary in termination of parental rights case and noting the Court's "historical recognition that freedom of personal choice in matters of family life is a fundamental liberty interest protected by the Fourteenth Amendment"); Parham v. J.R., 442 U.S. 584, 602, 61 L. Ed. 2d 101, 118, 99 S. Ct. 2493, 2504 (1979) (stating that "our jurisprudence historically has reflected [**531] Western civilization concepts of the family as a unit with broad parental authority [***27] over minor children"). In light of this extensive [*473] precedent, the Court in Troxel concluded that "□it cannot now be doubted that the Due Process Clause of the Fourteenth Amendment protects the fundamental right of parents to make decisions concerning the care, custody, and control of their children." Troxel, 530 U.S. at , 147 L. Ed. 2d at 57, 120 S. Ct. at 2060.

Section 607(b)(1) allows grandparents to petition for court-ordered visitation with the grandchildren when both parents have decided not to allow such visitation. By allowing the State to interfere with the parents' decision in this regard, section 607(b)(1) impinges upon the fundamental constitutional right of parents to make decisions regarding the upbringing of their children.

The State and the grandmother, Gail Lulay, argue that, even if section 607(b)(1) impinges upon a fundamental right, the statute does not significantly interfere with the fundamental right, and therefore, we should apply the rational basis test in reviewing the constitutionality of section 607(b)(1). See R.G., 131 Ill. 2d at 343 (stating that only statutes that "significantly interfere" with a fundamental right [***28] are subject to strict scrutiny), citing Zablocki v. Redhail, 434 U.S. 374, 386-88, 54 L. Ed. 2d 618, 630-31, 98 S. Ct. 673, 681-82 (1978). The State contends that section 607(b)(1) does not give grandparents the absolute right to visitation. Rather, the statute merely creates a procedure by which grandparents may petition for visitation under certain circumstances. The State points out that section 607(b)(1) states only that a court "may grant reasonable visitation privileges" (emphasis added) (750 ILCS 5/607(b)(1) (West 1998)) and that the grandparents have the burden of proving that visitation is in the child's best interests and welfare.

In light of the nature of the fundamental right at stake, the State's and the grandmother's argument is not persuasive. Encompassed within the well-established fundamental right of parents to raise their children is [*474] the right to determine with whom their children should associate. See Hoff v. Berg, 1999 ND 115, 595 N.W.2d 285, 291 (N.D. 1999) (stating that "deciding when, under what conditions, and with whom their children may associate is among the most important rights and [***29] responsibilities of parents," in holding that its most recent grandparent visitation statute was unconstitutional). It is the role of parents to nurture their children and to influence and shape their children's character. As the United States Supreme Court has recognized, "it is cardinal with us that the custody, care and nurture of the child reside first in the parents, whose primary function and freedom include preparation for obligations the state can neither supply nor hinder."

Prince v. Massachusetts, 321 U.S. 158, 166, 88 L. Ed. 645, 652, 64 S. Ct. 438, 442 (1944). This "preparation for obligation" includes the parents' determination of who will be instrumental in the development of their child's personality and character. Section 607(b)(1) allows the State to usurp the decisionmaking function of parents with respect to the relationships that their children will have. This decisionmaking function lies at the core of parents' liberty interest in the care, custody, and control of their children. To hold that section 607(b)(1) is not a significant interference with the fundamental right of parents to raise their children would be to effectively obliterate that [***30] fundamental right.

The significant interference that section 607(b)(1) has on parents' fundamental right is further evidenced by the procedure contemplated by the statute. The grandparents may file a petition for visitation under certain circumstances; in this case, where the parents are divorced. The parent or parents are then haled into court. The parents must presumably hire attorneys, and then present evidence and [**532] defend their decision regarding the visitation before a trial court. The parents' authority over their children is necessarily diminished by [*475] this procedure. This can only be characterized as a significant interference with parents' fundamental right to make decisions regarding the upbringing of their children. Indeed, □the "burden of litigating a domestic relations proceeding can itself be 'so disruptive of the parent-child relationship that the constitutional right of a custodial parent to make certain basic determinations for the child's welfare becomes implicated.' " Troxel, 530 U.S. at , 147 L. Ed. 2d at 62, 120 S. Ct. at 2065, quoting 530 U.S. at , 147 L. Ed. 2d at 78, 120 S. Ct. at 2079 (Kennedy, J., dissenting).

SOME IMPORTANT STATISTICS

* **63%** of youth suicides are from fatherless homes

(Source: U.S. D.H.K.S., Bureau of Census)

* **90%** of all homeless and runaway children are from fatherless homes (Source: U.S- D.H.H.S., Bureau of Census)

***85%** of all children that exhibit behavioral disorders come from fatherless homes (Source: Center for Disease Control)

***80%** of rapists motivated with displaced anger come from fatherless homes (Source: Criminal Justice & Behavior,Vol 14, p- 403-26, 1978)

***71%** of all high school dropouts come from fatherless homes

(Source: National Principals Association Report on the State of High schools)

***75%** of all adolescent patients in chemical abuse centers come from fatherless homes (Source: Rainbows For All God's Children.)

***70%** of juveniles in state-operated institutions come from fatherless homes

(Source: U.S. Dept. of Justice, Special Report,Sept 1988**These statistics translate to mean that children from a fatherless home are:**

***5** times more likely to commit suicide.

***32** times more likely to run away.

***20** times more likely to have behavioral disorders.

***14** times more likely to commit rape

***9** times more likely to drop out of high school.

***10** times more likely to abuse chemical substances.

***9** times more likely to end up in a state-operated institution.

***20** times more like to end up in prison.

The U.S. Census Bureau has reported that fathers with joint custody **pay 90.2% of all child support ordered**; fathers with limited visitation rights pay 79.1%.

THE AUTHOR:

RONALD L. ISAACS, J.D.

Mr. Isaacs is the father of five girls. Isaacs obtained his Bachelor's and Juris Doctorate degrees from Southern Illinois University.

A Vietnam veteran and retired member of the US Naval Reserve , Isaacs entered the practice of Law in 1987, after being involved in a lengthy custody and visitation battle himself.

Isaacs has developed a uniquely successful system of litigation that has resulted in many fathers winning custody , increased visitation rights and lower child support payments. He has turned false allegations of child abuse around against the false accuser in custody cases. He puts forth his system in several books for fathers. Mr. Isaacs' books include *The Multi-State Guide to Fathers' Rights*, *How to Minimize Child Support* (tactics also apply to Alimony), *Fighting False Allegations of Domestic Violence and Child Abuse*, the *Divorce/Custody Kit* (with *Visitation and Support Logbook).* All are available at **http://www.courttips.com.** Mr. Isaacs has appeared as guest on the **O'Reilly Factor, Queen Latifah Show, MSNBC,** and several other TV shows and radio programs. He hosted his own series called *Legal Tips* on nationwide television. He currently resides in Baton Rouge, Louisiana and handles cases in several states, primarily in Illinois. His web site is **http://www.dadslawyer.com.** He can practice in any state when affiliated with a local counsel.

FATHERS' RIGHTS RESOURCES

Multi-State Guide to Fathers' Rights	**$25.00**
How to Minimize Support	**$25.00**
Fighting False Allegations	**$25.00**
Visitation and Support Logbook	**$25.00**
Divorce/Custody Kit Comprehensive Guide to Fathers' Rights (includes all four books above)	**$75.00**

COURTROOM CONDUCT VIDEO..........$50.00 How to testify and act in court
HOW TO STOP A DIVORCE VIDEO.......$50.00

If you can find an attorney with the information in these books, his hourly charge would be much more than the price of these books. Mr. Isaacs' hourly fee is $250. You would have to spend several hours with him to gain this same information.

Order online at **http://www.fathers-rights.com** or call **(225) 766-0707** and order with your Mastercard or Visa credit card. All orders are shipped the next business day.

xxxxxxxxxxxxxxxxxxxxxxxxxxxxxxxxxxxxxxxxxxxx

DISCOUNT COUPON

THIS COUPON ENTITLES YOU TO A $10.00 DISCOUNT ON ANY ORDER OF ANY FATHERS' RIGHTS BOOK LISTED OR ON http://www.fathers-rights.com.

MAIL TO:

Fathers' Rights Foundation
10325 Winterhue Drive,
Baton Rouge, LA. 70810

XXXXXXXXXXXXXXXXXXXXXXXXXXXXXX